Bronislaw Malinowski's Concept of Law

Mateusz Stępień
Editor

Bronislaw Malinowski's Concept of Law

Springer

Editor
Mateusz Stępień
Department of Sociology of Law
Jagiellonian University
Krakow, Poland

ISBN 978-3-319-82481-9 ISBN 978-3-319-42025-7 (eBook)
DOI 10.1007/978-3-319-42025-7

Softcover reprint of the hardcover 1st edition 2016

Printed on acid-free paper

This Springer imprint is published by Springer Nature
The registered company is Springer International Publishing AG Switzerland

Preface

Bronislaw Malinowski is undoubtedly one of the titans of modern social sciences. It is impossible to underestimate his impact on a number of disciplines beyond social anthropology, including linguistics, religion, sociology or Cultural Studies, to name a few. Scientific legacy of Malinowski was mostly well-preserved and documented, as well as widely discussed—his works of magic, language, kinship, family, or religion became the subject of numerous studies. Moreover, his meta-conceptions (e.g. functionalism, cultural determinism) strongly influenced the debates on the way of practicing social science and mutual relationship between culture and biology. In broader terms, the importance of Malinowski's ideas exceeds the scope of social anthropology and it constitutes a part of the common heritage of social sciences.

Against this background, it is astonishing how little attention was paid to Malinowski's legal conceptions. Without a doubt, the author of *Argonauts* was popular and is still quoted among anthropologists interested in law. But even among them his legal thought has not been accurately reconstructed; hence, it may look unintelligible or even incomprehensible for readers (for which Malinowski is partly to blame). It is also important to note that Malinowski's legal thought has never been considered significant or truly groundbreaking in any sense within social anthropology. Unfortunately, the reception of his legal conceptions within legal sciences shared similar fate. With the exception of American legal realists, Malinowski was never recognized by legal scholars (including those with theoretically-oriented approaches) as one of the greatest authors within social sciences.

Trying to explain the marginalization of Malinowski's legal thought, it's easy to assume that law was never a central topic of his scientific interests. But a more detailed analysis of his scientific output reveals how much he wrote about law. With greater or lesser intensity he has been writing about law for years until his untimely death in early-1940s. Let us take a quick look at Malinowski's works concerning law before we move forward. In February 1923 Malinowski delivered a lecture before the Royal Institution of Great Britain on the forms of primitive law on The Triobriand Islands, published in 1925 under the title *The Forces of Law and Order in a Primitive Community*. More generalized arguments on law can be found in two short texts published in *Nature—Review of: Primitive Law by E. Sidney Hartland* (1925) and *Primitive Law and Order* (1926). The culmination of Malinowski's years of study on primitive law was a monograph published the same year (1926) under the title *Crime and Custom in Savage Society*. It is worth noting that it was the first book on (primitive) law based on ethnographic field research. Within *Crime and Custom* Malinowski referred to discussions on primitive law, relying on strong theoretical assumptions (including especially the functionalist approach) that led him to developing a project of new social anthropology, which requires, among other things, starting a new research on "the somewhat neglected subject of law" (1929). Such a conclusion was preceded by a section entitled *Theory of Primitive Law*. In 1934, in response to rising criticism leveled against his theory, Malinowski wrote a paper, published later as a comprehensive introduction to the monograph of Herbert I. Hogbin. In the second half of the 1930s Malinowski wrote *The Origins and Function of Law*, which remains unpublished to this day. However, he continued this line of research during his stay in the United States. During the early 1940s, Malinowski was giving seminars on primitive law and primitive jurisprudence at Yale University, from which interesting information can be obtained about his legal ideas. Numerous legal threads also appear in his last article—*A New Instrument for the Study of Law – Especially Primitive* (1942)—a kind of mini-manifesto on the subject of law. Although all aforementioned works are devoted entirely to law, legal threads can be found in many other fragments of Malinowski's work. Moreover, his approach to social world, in versions outlined both in *Argonauts* and in unfinished *A Scientific Theory of Culture*, has important implications for the general understanding of law.

This volume aims to fill the gap that arose as a result of a surprising lack of interest in Malinowski's legal conceptions. That goal is achieved by presenting the intellectual context in which Malinowski's legal thought has developed, as well as through a wider holistic reconstruction of his legal ideas. This book is organized into two parts. Part I consists of chapters that present the works of two outstanding Cracow Professors of law, who influenced Malinowski's legal thought. Part II reconstructs a more contextual understanding of his legal thought, and even develops his conceptions on the basis of modern research findings.

Chapter 1, *Not So Long Time Ago Before Malinowski... The Puzzle of Lotar Dargun's Influence on Bronislaw Malinowski*, attempts to sketch the intellectual background of Cracow, where young Malinowski was growing up. Michał Dudek reconstructs the thought of Lotar Dargun (1853–1893), a Cracow professor of law who was also interested in legal ethnography. Although Dudek clearly emphasizes the difficulties in determining whether there was any direct ("strong") impact of Dargun's ideas on young Malinowski, his reflections bring a fresh look at the intellectual environment, in which Malinowski grew up.

In Chap. 2, *Stanisław Estreicher: The Forgotten Master of Bronislaw Malinowski*, Krzysztof Pałecki explores the conceptions of another law professor from Cracow, Stanisław Estreicher (1869–1939), and considers his potential impact on young Malinowski. He argues that it was Estreicher who became a true master for the author of *Argonauts* and with whom he shared a similar vision of social world. Pałecki reconstructs so called "legal essentialism", or a set of assumptions Estreicher applied to primitive law, and investigates if Malinowski also shared them. From the perspective of biographical studies on Malinowski this is an innovative approach, because it complements a discussion with new information and interpretations that are essential for understanding the evolution of Malinowski's "intellectual base".

Chapter 3, *Malinowski's Multidimensional Conception of Law: Beyond Common Misunderstandings*, focuses on holistic, contextual reading of Malinowski's legal ideas against the background of his general assumptions about the knowing the social world. The author (Mateusz Stępień) argues that inconsistent and disordered ideas of Malinowski can be reconstituted into a cohesive conception of law as a multidimensional phenomenon. According to his thesis, Malinowski considered law as a phenomenon existing simultaneously at the biological, social and psychological level.

Chapter 4, *Bronislaw Malinowski and the Anthropology of Law*, aims to explain Malinowski's unique approach to law by confronting it with the dominant approaches both in legal science and within non-legal anthropological reflection. Tomáš Ledvinka treats the author of *Argonauts* as "a disciplinary Other", which allows him to identify the causes of misunderstanding of his legal concepts and to recognize the innovative nature of his ideas. In the second part of the chapter the methodological innovations of Malinowski's thought are discussed: cross-cultural comparison and participant observation. The chapter attempts to restore the lost significance of his legal conceptions that were unjustly marginalized.

Chapter 5, *Reciprocity as a Species of Fairness: Completing Malinowski's Theory of Law*, covers the problem of reciprocity in Malinowski's legal thought. The author of *Coral Gardens* distinguished civil from criminal law and explained the former as emerging organically out of social reciprocity. As James M. Donovan argues, the problem resulted from "inappropriate unit of analysis" used by Malinowski in forging a unified theory of law. It is the argument of the chapter that Malinowski's approach to law may be completed by recognizing that reciprocity should be considered as biologically rooted and culturally modified fairness. According to Donovan, so-called "altruistic punishment" allows considering (fairness-based) reciprocity also as the basis of criminal law.

This monograph began to take shape at a workshop: *Malinowski's Concept of Law from the Native's Point of View*, organized in Cracow by Jagiellonian University (on 12–13th September 2014) as an initiative to start a substantial debate on Malinowski's forgotten legal concepts. The event commemorated the 130th anniversary of his birth.

Krakow, Poland Mateusz Stępień

Contents

Part I

Chapter 1
Not So Long Time Ago Before Malinowski: The Puzzle of Lotar Dargun's Influence on Bronislaw Malinowski

Michał Dudek

1.1 Introduction

Many people interested in the work of Bronislaw Malinowski (1884–1942) may look at the title of this chapter and start wondering what Lotar Dargun (1853–1893) is doing in the context of elaboration of Malinowski's legacy concerning law and legal issues, forming the main goal of this volume. Keeping in mind this possible wonderment, one must remember that scholars on Malinowski, who meticulously study not only his scientific achievements but also his biography, state that Dargun can be regarded as one of few Polish scholars who influenced Malinowski, at least at the early stage of his research (Kubica 1986, p. 145; Paluch 1988, p. 5; see also Thornton and Skalník 1993, pp. 61–63; Stępień 2014, pp. 405–406). Moreover, Malinowski himself made references, often in a positive tone, to Dargun (1913, pp. 179, 180, 181, 184; 1930, p. 24; 1962, p. 13; 1993, pp. 250, 257–258) and even commented, in a critical manner, on his one particular idea (1913, pp. 188, 189, 201).

After this short reminder, those who are wondering why Dargun is recalled in context of Malinowski, get a partial answer to their question. It is only partial because knowing that some say that Dargun influenced Malinowski does not equal knowing what exactly Dargun researched and why his work may be considered important for Malinowski and how to understand the thesis about his influence on one of the most important and famous twentieth-century anthropologists. The aim of this chapter is, for the first time in English literature, to try to present and discuss a significant part of Dargun's work, which seems to be relevant from the perspective of Malinowski's own achievements, and problematize, even question the validity of thesis that Dargun influenced Malinowski.

M. Dudek (✉)
Department of Sociology of Law, Jagiellonian University, Krakow, Poland
e-mail: michal.dudek@uj.edu.pl

M. Stępień (ed.), *Bronislaw Malinowski's Concept of Law*,
DOI 10.1007/978-3-319-42025-7_1

The originality of the project undertaken in this chapter needs some explanation. Although there are some references, comments and even reviews of Dargun's work in English literature, they are very perfunctory (Smith 1893; Schott 1982, pp. 56–57; Wagner-Hasel 2003, p. 155; Davies 2010, pp. 82–84; Eller 2011, pp. 133, 149–150, 159–160, 174). Because Dargun published only in Polish and German—often the first versions of his works were presented in Polish, then in German—his work is better (but definitely not thoroughly) known among Polish and German-language scholars. Still, he can be considered, without any exaggeration, as a nearly forgotten, undeservedly, scholar. Although the main goal here is to discuss the thesis about his influence on Malinowski, as already mentioned, the presented chapter is also a good occasion to try to remind and popularize Dargun and his work among wider, English-language audience. Moreover, the original character of this work comes from the emphasis on the methodology Dargun consistently used in his most important works. The way of thinking Dargun represented and proposed—a specific common denominator of many of his studies, which seem to be important from the perspective of Malinowski's own work—did not meet with as much interest as his other scientific achievements. Putting it under scrutiny is also a good way to try to address the issue of Dargun's influence on Malinowski.

The conclusion of this study is as follows. In the face of many details of Dargun's work, which seem to be relevant from the perspective of Malinowski's own scientific interests and achievements, the thesis that Dargun influenced Malinowski proves to be very vague and controversial—just puzzling. Namely, there are some significant differences in the way Dargun and Malinowski worked and thought, and in the goals they wanted to achieve with their research. Keeping in mind those differences one has to be either very careful and precise when arguing about the influence Dargun had on Malinowski—those who so far propose that thesis about the influence evidently do not justify it fully, hence the controversy—or simply give up with this argument. Assuming that Dargun is not known among English-language readers, as said earlier, one should begin with some basic information concerning his biography and his work.

1.2 Life of Lotar Dargun

In comparison to very rich resources on Malinowski's life, the details of Dargun's biography are very modest (K. 1893; Anonymous Press Note 1893a, b; Patkaniowski 1964a, b, pp. 226–228; Posner 1893a; Pol 2011; Żukowski 2014, pp. 76–77), so modest, that one can even say that most of his life remains today simply unknown. Nevertheless, what can be said about him for sure is that his life and consequently academic career was very short, unfortunately. Namely, Dargun was born on October 7, 1853 in Opava (now: Czech Republic; then: Duchy of Upper and Lower Silesia) and died of meningitis (some added that illness came from overwork) on April 29, 1893 in Krakow (now: Republic of Poland; then:

Grand Duchy of Krakow). In Krakow he attended gymnasium and after this stage of his education he went (1871) to study at the University of Vienna, where he earned a PhD degree in philosophy (history) (1877). Then, he came back to Krakow to study law at the Jagiellonian University and earned another PhD degree—this time, in law (1881). His academic career was devoted to this particular discipline and soon after PhD in law he earned Habilitation in law with a specialization in German law (1882). Since the academic year of 1882/1883 until his death in 1893 he continuously worked and lectured at the Jagiellonian University's Faculty of Law. Although Dargun got offers from other (German-language) universities, he devoted himself to Jagiellonian University, where soon he received extraordinary (1884) and full professorship (1888). As a Professor of History of Law and German Law—a predecessor of Stanisław Estreicher (1869–1939)—he was chosen to be a Dean of the Faculty of Law at the Jagiellonian University (1892/1893). The performance of this honorable function, as well as his highly original and impressive scientific research, was interrupted by his premature death.

1.3 Overview of Lotar Dargun's Work

Originality of Dargun's legacy comes from the fact that he was primarily and formally a historian of law focused on German law, but most of his work goes far beyond the commonly understood historical studies on the law, its particular institutions, their changes or receptions. Although his life was relatively short, he left quite a significant quantity of publications of a high quality, which allowed him to participate, on an equal footing, in international academic discourse at the time. His works are very diverse and their interdisciplinary character commands genuine appreciation, even today, when the denial of disciplinary boundaries is a common practice. In the face of this diversity and for the sake of clarity of presentation, one can classify Dargun's work as follows.

First, Dargun conducted research which can be named as strictly historical (legal-historical), in a "classical" (not ethnological) sense (1879a, 1888/1891, 1889). For instance, he was interested in the changes of Polish municipal law and penal law, mainly from the perspective of reception of famous *Constitutio Criminalis Carolina*. Although those works seem to be still remembered among some historians of law, he is definitely most well-known for his legal-ethnological analyses of some social institutions, which constituted a significant contribution to the ethnological jurisprudence (on that movement: generally, e.g. Post 1891; with explicit reference to Dargun, Schott 1982).

Within this legal-ethnological part of his work, Dargun presented a number of studies devoted to the analysis and explanation of such basic social (and simultaneously, legal) institutions like marriage (1879b), property (1880a, 1884c), inheritance (1880b), and lastly, kinship (Dargun 1882a, 1883a, 1891, 1892a), using ethnological data and historical sources of the law available at the time. In these works he introduced and carefully justified concepts and theses which challenged popular views on these institutions. For instance, Dargun can and should be remembered for criticizing the belief that at the early (even earliest) stages of development of human societies there was no individual property. Contrary to primitive communism thesis, Dargun argued that in fact in the so-called "savage" societies the individual property was first, primary. Communal forms of property emerged later, with the development and increase of complexity of societies.

Closely connected to these legal-ethnological studies of abovementioned institutions are Dargun's works devoted to the methodological issues (1883b, 1887). He was very self-conscious about the methodology, or, more generally speaking, way of thinking employed in analysis of basic social and legal institutions from the historical and ethnological perspective. It is also worth stressing that although studies on methodology are situated at a relatively early or middle period of the entire Dargun's oeuvre, he consistently followed his methodological proposal in his later (and final) legal-ethnological works.

However, Dargun did not limit himself to the abovementioned research areas. He also developed original concepts beyond the legal-historical or legal-ethnological studies and methodological reflections accompanying them. For instance, one has to remember and acknowledge Dargun's original contribution to political economy (1884a, 1885, 1890). Within this discipline, Dargun is known especially for proposing a highly original understanding of concepts of altruism and egoism. Originality of his approach to these issues comes from the fact that he wanted to separate concepts of altruism and egoism from purely subjective analysis of motives behind given actions undertaken by people. He tried to go beyond the distinction of altruism and egoism based on the broadly understood psychology (attitudes) of people whose actions are studied. Instead, he proposed objective accounts of altruism and egoism, using the criterion of the nearest goal of action. Accordingly, Dargun argued that the subject of analysis should be only the action and its first consequence—the nearest goal (objectively speaking). What is actually reached in the first place by the given actor—something beneficial for her/him or for other people—determines whether the certain action is egoistic or altruistic, regardless of the actor's motives. In other words, Dargun distinguished the actual goal of action (subjective, resulting from one's motives) and the nearest goal of action (objective, first consequence of it), and focused on the latter. Then, he employed this understanding to the analysis of some social institutions (not only family or property, which were constantly of Dargun's interest, but also public finances).

Next to such theoretical discussion on basic concepts of political economy, and their use in analysis of some actual institutions, Dargun worked on one particular social problem, lying on the intersection of such disciplines like sociology, political economy and law. He was not detached from social reality at the time and actually saw the important problem of the situation of working class. Dargun was particularly interested in legal instruments which were meant to protect workers from accidents and extensively published on that matter, with the emphasis on Austrian and German legislation (1884b, 1888).

Dargun's extensive work was not limited to the above-outlined threads. He was also deeply interested in subjects, which do not fit the presented categories. For instance, he carefully analyzed the problem of war (1892b). In the spirit similar to the mature functionalism, he showed the positive, constructive aspects of waging wars, for instance, in constituting nations through them, fulfilling an integrative function. In general, his approach to the problem of war can be summarized with idiom: "every cloud has a silver lining".

The outline of Dargun's work cannot be complete without mentioning his significant reviewing activity. Namely, he left behind many thorough reviews of academic publications, which were relevant for his interests (their exhaustive enumeration is unnecessary at this point). Even in a relatively concise form of review he managed to present his own original approach to the issue in question. Moreover, some of Dargun's shorter pieces of work, which formally can be classified as reviews, were in fact full-fledged academic essays (e.g. 1882b). At their occasion, Dargun also undertook the problems that went significantly beyond his main interests, like the issue of social knowledge of the law (1893).

1.4 What to Discuss in Context of Bronislaw Malinowski?

In the face of overview of Dargun's work, one might say "what a choice!". Indeed, keeping in mind the main subject of this chapter—the particular thesis on Dargun's influence on Malinowski, and not the entire Dargun's oeuvre—one has to narrow the planned analysis to some particular element in Dargun's work. To make and justify that choice, one should look first at the work of Malinowski himself. In the context of his achievements, Dargun's research on kinship is definitely the most important, because precisely this part of his legacy was the subject to explicit references and comments in the writings of Malinowski (1913, pp. 179, 180, 181, 184, 188, 189, 201; 1930, p. 24; 1993, pp. 250, 257–258; with a small exception of vague reference to Dargun's view on marriage: 1962, p. 13).

In his work on kinship Dargun consistently and even stubbornly defended the view that the kinship by mothers was historically the first, prior to the kinship by fathers. He justified this by stating that, *inter alia*, for representatives of the "savage", "primitive" peoples the fatherhood was uncertain, whereas biological relationship of mothers with their children was far more evident and uncontroversial. This led to a much closer relationship between the child and the woman's (mother's) male relatives, than between the child and its biological father and had many significant consequences on inheritance or marriage, which are shown by Dargun based on many legal-historical sources. However, in the light of the thesis of the primacy of kinship by mothers a problem arose. How to reconcile the maternal line with the commonly perceived predominance of men? Dargun was determined to keep his original thesis on the kinship. To do that, in his last works on kinship he explicitly proposed, what in his previous studies was only hinted—to distinguish relationships based on kinship (*Verwandtschaft*) and those based on power (*Gewalt*). This in turn gave him four categories, which can be used to analyze different societies at different stages of development, namely: kinship by mothers, kinship by fathers, relationships in which power belongs to women and relationships in which power belongs to men. Dargun argued that in a given society there can be, for example, simultaneously kinship by mothers and predominance of men (power belongs to men). In other words, according to Dargun the particular kinds of kinship relationships and power relationships are not mutually exclusive. Although some combinations may seem contradictory (like just mentioned kinship by mothers and men's power), Dargun argued that they actually occurred.

This a bit more elaborated reminder of part of Dargun's legacy is needed in the context of thesis that Dargun influenced Malinowski. The distinction between kinship and power is precisely the only part of Dargun's work which was commented (and not only referred to) by Malinowski. In *The Family Among Australian Aborigines. A Sociological Study* he bluntly said that the reminded distinction is simply flawed for two reasons.

First, Malinowski (1913, pp. 188, 189, 201) argued that Dargun (1892a) mistakenly understood kinship only as an objective, physiological relationship—consanguinity. Malinowski (1913, p. 182) quite clearly stated that this approach is insufficient for social analysis. The mere biological fact of 'the physiological bond of common blood' between given persons is not all what the concept of kinship should encompass. For Malinowski this objective relationship is only a "starting point" to properly grasp the problem of kinship. It seems that for him kinship is a specific conjunction of objective, physiological fact and its 'social acknowledgment and interpretation'. Malinowski in his first monograph accused Dargun of lacking this particular subtlety.

But it was not the only reason of critique of Dargun's distinction between kinship and power. In the commented work of Malinowski he seemed to accuse Dargun's idea of making the concept of power way too analytical. In particular he (1913, p. 188) criticized it for not considering the elements of (physiological) kinship in its own (power's) definition.

However, one might say that Malinowski had a point and Dargun's distinction was artificial and too sterile in the face of the actual complexity of phenomena he was trying to grasp, but there are some significant problems with assessment of Malinowski's critique; whether he actually was right. Namely, it may be controversial whether Dargun in fact consistently identified kinship (*Verwandtschaft*) with consanguinity (*Blutsverwandtschaft*) in a way Malinowski presented. In fact, Malinowski (1913, pp. 188–189) himself gave examples of Dargun's argumentation where he seemed to transcend his own distinction, at least its reconstruction provided and criticized by Malinowski. Moreover, in one of his last works Dargun (1891, p. 240) said clearly that the natural bond of blood serves as a 'substrate' of kinship. The use of this particular notion—substrate—would then suggest that Dargun was aware of the problem with identifying kinship only with blood bonds. However, by saying that bond of blood is a substrate of kinship—its basis; something which gives a beginning to it, but does not equal it—he seemed to avoid this problem and leave room for more complicated accounts of kinship, similar to those proposed by Malinowski. But, as the latter showed, although there are passages in Dargun's work where he actually went beyond criticized strictly physiological understanding of kinship, in his writings he was mostly using the concept of bond of blood. Because of that the question arises: did Dargun in fact identify kinship only with biological relationship—as most of his wording suggests—or maybe he actually had much more wider and complex assumptions about kinship—this suspicion is justified by the notion of substrate—but Dargun simply did not keep bringing them back in his texts, wherever it would be needed, and consistently used shorter formulations, like bond of blood? This significant confusion is even deepened by later writings of Malinowski, in which he also referred to Dargun's work on kinship.

Just one year after the publication of *The Family Among Australian Aborigines. A Sociological Study*, in 1914 Malinowski published paper '*Soziologie der Familie*' ['*The Sociology of the Family*'] (1993—English translation). Whereas in 1913 he was highly critical, in 1914 he made a 180-degree turn in relation to Dargun's concepts and their assessment. Malinowski (1993, p. 258) explicitly referred to Dargun's distinction between kinship and power, but this time there was not even a slightest trace of previous critique. Malinowski praised Dargun's 'ingenious and thorough analyses' of kinship and even said something which in a way contradicted his criticisms published in 1913:

> Dargun analyzes the concepts of 'power' [*Gewalt*] and 'kinship' and demonstrates that no constants correspond universally to identical social realities, but that in every case the totality of the jural concepts and social institutions must be taken into consideration in order to ascertain how the kinship relations of a people are constituted. Dargun's criticism of the concepts of kinship, his deep insight into the functional dependence of the kinship relations on jural, moral and economic factors, and on the general structure of the respective society, have, besides their direct value as contributions to the problem in question, also an even more general value as a guide for the future direction of scientific sociology in the proper sense of the word (Malinowski 1993, p. 258).

Precisely this passage is particularly baffling from the perspective of Malinowski's monograph from 1913. In it, Dargun's understanding of kinship was criticized because it was (allegedly) too dependent on one objective, physiological factor—actual bond of blood. Whereas in 1914, it was praised for showing intertwinement of kinship with many other distinguishable factors. Keeping in mind that Malinowski's recalled studies could have been in fact written in different chronological order than order indicated by their years of publication, it is extremely difficult to fully explain presented change of mind. Solution similar to famous Althusserian epistemological break seems to be way too radical and unnecessary in the discussed context. Independently of many other hypothetical explanations, for example, insufficiently precise narrative of Dargun, linguistic misunderstanding or Malinowski's closer and more careful reading of Dargun, including his works in Polish and initial explanation of the concept of kinship with the notion of substrate, one thing seems to be certain. The presented one and only instance of Malinowski's discussion of Dargun (not just references to him) is on the one hand way too detailed and specific and on the other way too vague and confusing to use it as a starting point for analysis of the thesis about Dargun's influence on Malinowski. Malinowski himself focused only on one particular thread from the diverse work of Dargun. Moreover, he did that in a rather general, perfunctory and confusing manner. For this reason, another point of departure should be chosen to discuss the thesis in question.

As already mentioned, Malinowski also referred to Dargun in context of analysis of marriage (1962, p. 13). This reference is in turn so vague, that it definitely cannot be used as a proper starting point to discuss the main problem here—the (alleged) influence of Dargun on Malinowski. Similarly, most of other highly specialized Dargun's works seem to be inappropriate to assess a rather general issue, which is the subject of scrutiny in this chapter.

Fortunately, there is a way to overcome this impasse. One can try to present the general methodology, way of thinking Dargun consistently used in his legal-ethnological inquiry. As said earlier, this is the common denominator for this part of Dargun's oeuvre, which is also definitely the closest to the interests and work of Malinowski himself. An attempt to take a closer look at the general structure of the most significant part of Dargun's legacy seems to be useful not only in the context of thesis about the influence on Malinowski. It is also an original project in its own right, because Dargun's legal-ethnological methodology was not discussed even by his contemporaries, who analyzed his work soon after his premature death (Jaworski 1893; Posner 1893b; Potkański 1893). Therefore, there is a gap, which should be fulfilled.

Accordingly, the following part is devoted to the presentation of Dargun's way of thinking, as it was described by him in his programmatic paper '*O zastosowaniu etnografii do historyi prawa*' ['*On the Use of Ethnography in History of Law*'] (1883b; the programmatic character of this study is confirmed by Jaworski 1893, p. 581, footnote 17 and Patkaniowski 1964a, pp. 361–362). Dargun followed his methodological proposal in his legal-ethnological studies, the ones which are, objectively speaking, the most relevant from the perspective of Malinowski and, subjectively speaking, were in fact read and commented (at least some of them) by Malinowski, as shown earlier. The presentation below is the basis for discussion on validity of thesis that Dargun influenced Malinowski, which also includes some more general remarks on Dargun's work. However, before proceeding to these critical analyses, it is necessary to recapitulate the basics of Dargunian approach to legal-ethnological research.

1.5 Lotar Dargun's Way of Thinking: Presentation

Dargun began the presentation of his way of thinking by statement that observation is an appropriate starting point for conducting any research (with exception of mathematics and theology) (1883b, p. 15). Then he showed he had a quite peculiar (or maybe not) view on human history. According to him, everything has its previous cause and the whole history can be regarded as a chain of syllogisms, but the first premises are simply unknown (1883b, p. 16). That is why he was quite suspicious about some generalizations made based on historical or legal-historical sources, even the ones significantly old. For instance, these sources, available at the Dargun's lifetime, often depicted social reality in which there was a kinship by fathers and system of common property. Although they showed very old reality, for Dargun it did not mean that they actually presented the original, first versions of the relevant social and legal institutions (kinship, property, or marriage and inheritance). As already said, Dargun was deeply convinced that before kinship by fathers there was solely kinship by mothers and before common there was individual property. How he came to these conclusions, for which he is so well-known?

Dargun (1883b, p. 16) believed that progress in researching human history (including history of institutions) was possible because of the two disciplines: comparative linguistics and comparative ethnography. Dargun's use of the former was rather infrequent. There are some passages in his legal-ethnological studies, where he referred to certain findings of broadly understood linguistics. They were mostly fragments of folk poetry, where, for example, the indifference of fathers towards their biological children was quite evident and thus justified (in Dargun's view) the thesis that at some point there had to be other kinship system than kinship by fathers—kinship by mothers (1883b, p. 21).

Nevertheless, he was definitely more focused on the latter discipline—comparative ethnography. Its basic premise, according to Dargun (1883b, p. 16), was as follows. There are some universal features in human social organizations, which are common in so-called "savage", "primitive" societies as well as in so-called "civilized" societies. In those "civilized" ones one can find elements of strictly "savage" character and origin and conversely, "primitive" populations have "civilized" components, but in their early, "germinal" stage. Dargun (1883b, p. 17) added to that point that institutions of "savage" people can and actually evolve and institutions of "civilized" societies often can be explained only through reference to their "savage" origin. Certainly, a significant question arose in the face of this general assumption. How to determine the earlier, more "savage" stages of development of "civilized" peoples and their institutions? Dargun (1883b, p. 17) believed that there are some universals, or, to use his own words, that there is 'sameness of main features' in human social organizations. He (1883b, p. 17) said that 'there have to be some expressions of culture which are tightly connected to the human nature' and are in fact its and only its consequence, and not a result of any other influences (external conditions and factors). His legal-ethnological works are filled with many examples of similarities across the globe and time in various human populations. On their basis, he formulated thesis that those similarities are not from some accident/chance or historical connection. They come from universal human nature. In other words, comparative ethnography according to Dargun's (1883b, p. 17) own statement and basically most of his legal-ethnological work is "simply" to look at contemporary "savage" peoples, based on the available empirical data, as if they are representations of the forgotten past of the "civilized" peoples; when they were "savage" as well.

It seems then that whole legal-ethnological (relevant from the perspective of Malinowski) work of Dargun can be described as realization of explanation procedure, which is pretty simple when one thinks about it more carefully. Namely, Dargun wanted to know how the ancestors of "civilized" peoples were actually organized in a given respect; how come that some of their social and legal institutions were so peculiar, even bizarre, as they are described in historical or legal-historical sources, for instance, famous passages from Tacitus' *Germania* on preference of nephews over sons as hostages. This is the *explanandum*. On the other hand, as the *explanans* Dargun treated known (because of empirical fieldwork which was available to him) information on how the "savage" peoples are/were organized in a given respect. The underlying assumption of this explanation procedure is that the known "savage" people (or, to be more precise, details on their organization) are the reflections of the forgotten, unknown past of "civilized" people, from the stage when they also could be regarded as "savage". Naturally, Dargun (1883b, p. 17) was clear and admitted that with this method one cannot reach the farthest and oldest details—"The Beginning". Nevertheless, he (1883b, p. 18) was confident that some social institutions (their particular forms) which existed in the past simply could not vanish without any trace left. Accordingly, their "later" traces, residues can be explained only by their assumed "previous", "original" and "complete" manifestations. Sources of these specific assumptions about them, which are intended to fulfill gaps in historical testimonies, come from the broadly understood ethnological data (various descriptions of diverse "savage" peoples provided by travelers, traders or diverse scholars).

To properly understand Dargun's method, one should consider one of the many examples he presented (1883b, p. 20). According to one of the old-Danish laws, written down in thirteenth century, child born by the free woman is also free although the father was a slave and conversely—child born by a woman who is a slave is also a slave, although the father was free. Historical sources on old-Danish society available at the Dargun's lifetime were insufficient to answer the emerging question: why status of mothers was privileged in such a way? This was the *explanandum*. Dargun proposed to solve this riddle (and other similar, for example, relating to the cited fragment of *Germania*) by reference to the relatively much more recent testimonies on the social organization of various "savage" peoples. Ethnography research available to Dargun showed that among many different "primitive" societies there are/were many peculiarities and oddities similar to recalled case of old-Danish law, and those peculiarities are/were in fact the derivatives of kinship by mothers. This was the source of the *explanans*. Accordingly, Dargun explained this particular norm described in written set of old-Danish laws by saying that the referred society was or even had to be based on system of kinship by mothers—it was the only adequate explanation. He (1883b, p. 22) also added that before the application of comparative ethnography there were many unsuccessful attempts to explain institutions and laws objectively based on this form of kinship.

Presented general way of thinking was not only informed by the already described assumption that the known "primitive" societies are the reflections of the unknown past (because of the insufficiency of historical testimonies) of "civilized" peoples. Dargun (1883b, p. 19) was also using a specific biological analogy. The earlier the stage of development of different peoples, the more alike they are, similarly as animals of different species. For instance, embryos of different kinds of mammals are practically indistinguishable, but as they develop their distinctive features become increasingly more apparent. In Dargun's view, ethnography gives information about the earlier development stages of human societies based on the data on the "savage" peoples. This information can be then used to determine the earlier development stages of the particular "civilized" peoples, because of the assumed regularity in the biological analogy and in the belief in universal human nature.

Concluding this part, Dargun's way of thinking fits very well the following characterization of ethnological jurisprudence proposed by Albert Hermann Post (1839–1895), one of the most prominent representatives of that movement:

> Ethnological jurisprudence is (...) able to supply complementary information at a point where the threads of the history of law are lost in the obscurity of early times (...) The collecting of the laws of uncivilised peoples constitutes an independent task of ethnological jurisprudence. In this way the latter science will fill up the gaps which historical jurisprudential inquiry left open in our knowledge of the jural life of man (...) The discovery of ethnographical parallels led to wholly different ideas. It became clear that a great portion of human ethnical existence was not founded in the peculiar character of particular peoples, but in the character of the human race, in the universal nature of man (...) Especially deserving of consideration are the laws of the so-called savage peoples that have been so much neglected and contemned hitherto; since they bring to light the jural consciousness of humanity in its germinal stages, and since higher formations are invariably best understood when we know their first beginnings (Post 1891, pp. 34, 35, 37).

1.6 Lotar Dargun's Way of Thinking: Critical Remarks

Naturally, it is important to look at work of Dargun from the perspective of his times (Pol 2011, p. 476). Nevertheless, it seems valuable to try to present some critical remarks about his legal-ethnological research, some of which could have been even formulated at the time, before proceeding to the issue of Dargun's influence on Malinowski.

Dargun's method brings to mind a kind of meta-analysis. When he said about the observation method, one has to keep in mind that he in fact did not conduct any fieldwork himself. Dargun was representing quite a typical "arm-chair anthropology". He "simply" gathered many materials—as he admitted at one point (1880a, p. 122), mostly prepared by non-lawyers—and tried to use these information available at the time to prove some points about the basic social and legal institutions. In the end it always boiled down to the following reasoning (Jaworski 1893, p. 504). From the existence of some form of given institution among many contemporary "savage" peoples, Dargun inferred the existence of the very same form in the past of particular population (mostly it was about details on the past of Germanic peoples). On the one hand, he was a firm believer in appropriateness of observation as a research method, but on the other he personally did not use it, did not conduct any empirical research. He was "only" using the results of observation of other people, who also represented a wide array of disciplines and intellectual backgrounds, and were in fact conducting their research (or "research") in very different ways. The way of thinking Dargun proposed could then lead to incorrect results.

Although Dargun stressed at many occasions the inductiveness of the method he employed (e.g., 1882a, pp. 254, 350; 1883b, pp. 18, 22, 37; see also Jaworski 1893, p. 500; Potkański 1893, p. 125; Pol 2011, p. 475), the narrative in his work is definitely qualitative, in the very soft sense. His works are filled with enormous amount of diverse examples, which seem to be poorly ordered and selected in accordance with the criterion, which for the reader seems to be unclear. Moreover, his analyses can be regarded as a good example of verificationism, not falsificationism, in the Popperian sense. Dargun was focused on the data which confirmed his theses, and although he was aware of few empirical testimonies contradicting his views, he seemed to treat them fairly flippantly, if not simply ignored them (e.g. Dargun 1882a, p. 254). It must be remembered though that such seemed to be the intellectual climate at the time, according to which 'proved [theses—M.D.] prove the power of talent' (Jaworski 1893, p. 500). It blends well with another remark which comes to mind.

Dargun can also be interpreted as a searcher for the best explanation of peculiarities which can be found in various historical and legal-historical sources, like the recalled fragment of *Germania* or old-Danish legal rule written down in thirteenth century. Indeed, these and other surprising testimonies seem to simply fit the thesis about the kinship by mothers, but one has to keep in mind the following issue, which is trivial only on the surface. That something seems to be the consequence or derivative of particular hypothetical premise does not necessarily make this premise true. Dargun faced the extremely complex issues, which were accompanied by constantly growing literature and emergence and evolution of specialized discipline. Although, in the light of the coming of new findings, he was updating his achievements, for example, by returning to the issue of kinship, but still he often sounded as overly confident and uncritical towards his own vision.

There are also other controversies coming from various extremely strong and in fact dubious assumptions Dargun took. In the first place, he stressed that there must be similarity, even sameness between "savage" peoples, which are the subject of testimonies he used, and "savage" ancestors of "civilized" peoples, who were not described in historical sources, thus the gap Dargun wanted to fulfill. Certainly, this similarity is the consequence of the more general assumption/faith in universal human nature. Not only it is controversial, but also very simplistic and may in the end lead to trivialization of research.

Another problem is connected with the criteria of first-next forms of given institutions and distinction of various stages of development of human societies (this problem is noticed by Jaworski 1893, p. 571). In the face of Dargun's argumentation one might ask a question: why exactly something is classified as first, primal or simpler and something else as next, more developed and complex? Similar is the case with the assumption that social institutions which existed in the past simply could not vanish without any trace left. Here the doubt can take the form of following question: but what about some revolutions which could erase the given stage of certain society and a particular form of institution, which are hinted by Dargun (1883b, p. 18)?

Additionally, when Dargun referred to some sources of law (like the mentioned old-Danish rule), he seemed to assume that the extralegal social norms in a given analyzed society (norms actually observed by their addressees) were simply consistent with legal norms described in the written source he was using. In other words, it seems dubious, not only from today's perspective, to infer the (alleged) true picture of social practice in a given aspect from the contents of written sources of law. Namely, there can be, actually are and probably were some significant discrepancies between law in historical written sources and law in the past actual practice. Although in different sources there are descriptions of certain norms or the exact legal provisions it does not mean that in the given analyzed society a rule in question was actually followed. However, Dargun seemed to be too strongly attached to vision according to which laws in legal-historical sources are simply the generalized descriptions of what representatives of given society were actually doing. Consequently, he did not see the problem of the mentioned discrepancies and that the historical sources of law do not have to show an actual social practice.

1.7 Puzzle

Naturally, these relatively loose comments do not constitute all the possible points for discussion about Dargun. He definitely deserves a more thorough presentation and analysis. Nevertheless, the presented methodology he was using in his legal-ethnological research and critical remarks on it may be used to problematize the thesis that Dargun influenced Malinowski, provoke to carefully rethink it.

First, trying to compare these two, one might say that Dargun was in fact the "arm-chair" researcher of "the Near". He simply wanted to understand why the institutions of peoples relatively close to what he identified with (European populations) are/were the way they are/were by tracing their alleged previous, more basic forms from various information on "savage" peoples, who he believed reflected earlier development stages of populations he was actually most interested in, like Germanic peoples. Dargun only used, not in uncontroversial manner, information on mostly non-European peoples as a way of explaining some peculiarities he found in historical and legal-historical sources on European populations (their ancestors). Moreover, keeping in mind the belief in universal human nature and the specific biological analogy he was using, it is even possible to say that Dargun only formally was working on the differences among cultures and ethnic groups but in fact he was researching human social institutions in general. Ultimately, the observed differences were not some inherent differences, but simple derivatives of differences mostly in time (stage of development), but also in space (characteristics of inhabited environment).

On the other hand, Malinowski significantly differed from Dargun. Indeed, at the early stage of his career he was "arm-chair anthropologist", but soon he drastically changed his approach. He started conducting a meticulous fieldwork, during which he was very self-aware about methodology employed, how to interpret what he actually and personally observed. He was carefully gathering information on local people, which, as he convincingly showed, itself was a highly demanding task. Dargun treated such data as only a starting point for his analyses which were in fact aimed at understanding mostly historical European legal peculiarities. For Dargun the knowledge about "savage" peoples was only a mean, not an end in itself. In comparison to him, Malinowski was a researcher of "the Far" who actually wanted to know and understand representatives of cultures other than his own and was perfectly aware that it is scientific goal in its own right. Certainly, in the entire Malinowski's oeuvre the ambitions to generalize, to create full-fledged theory of culture are quite evident. It leads in turn to another difference in relation to Dargun. He did not seem to want to create similar abstract theory, which would aim to encompass culture and social life in general, at least one cannot clearly see such an aspiration in his published works.

Keeping in mind these most evident and important differences between Dargun and Malinowski—differences in goals, methods or approaches and ambitions—the thesis that the former influenced the latter is very baffling. From the perspective of Dargun's general legal-ethnological methodology it is extremely difficult to actually see impact he could have on Malinowski. Certainly, this puzzle can be addressed in few ways.

Anyone who formulates similar thesis should specify the used understanding of notion of influence. Malinowski attended so many lectures, met so many intellectuals during his studies in Krakow (e.g. Kubica 1986), not to mention the whole of his lifetime, that it is extremely demanding and in fact quite risky to say that someone had influence on him, which was more evident and important, than any other person whom Malinowski met or read. Such a claim must then have a very strong foundation, which is simply missing in the commented case of Dargun. Moreover, one can say that there are larger and smaller or very important and almost insignificant influences and these distinctions also should be included in the detailed thesis. One might venture to say that without such a specification the statement that one person influenced the other does not mean anything.

Furthermore, one can argue that Dargun's influence on Malinowski was not direct but through intermediary, for which Estreicher could be considered. As said earlier, he was a successor of Dargun in the Department of German Law at the Jagiellonian University. Estreicher knew Dargun personally and through his work (e.g. Estreicher 1895; 1902, pp. 250, 251, 256, 281), and definitely can be regarded as being under his influence (e.g. Patkaniowski 1964b, p. 227). For instance,

Estreicher in his work on the beginnings of contract law used the same biological, "embryonic" analogy Dargun was using (compare Dargun 1883b, p. 19 and Estreicher 1902, p. 239). Thus, if the relationship between Estreicher and Malinowski is far more clear (e.g. Patkaniowski 1964b, p. 233; see also Chap. 2) than between Dargun and Malinowski, then maybe it is possible that Estreicher transferred some idea (or ideas) of Dargun to Malinowski, in more or less modified form. However, this way of addressing the commented issue is not complete. There are still significant discrepancies between Dargun and Malinowski, which were outlined above. Moreover, it is unclear exactly what from the Dargun's doctrine affected Estreicher and, through him, Malinowski.

There is also another approach, which might be taken in the face of highlighted differences between Dargun and Malinowski. If the thesis about Dargun's influence on Malinowski proves to be very vague, unclear, insufficiently justified and simply controversial, in the light of analysis above, then maybe one should give up this argument. This solution is definitely easier than sticking to some form of thesis about the influence, but at the same time appears to be much better justified. However, for the sake of scholarly integrity one should not rule out the other way (or ways) of addressing the problem of Dargun's influence on Malinowski, which can bring different results than the presented argumentation. In reference to the already suggested issue of notion of influence, one can describe the analysis proposed in this chapter as based on very strong understanding of that concept. According to it one might say about the influence when one scholar shares basically the same general research philosophy and methodology with the other scholar, who is considered by the former as a source of inspiration to take given approach. As seen, this particular assumption leads to negative evaluation of thesis about Dargun's influence on Malinowski. However, one might as well take a rather soft understanding of notion of influence and argue, for instance, that it is already justified to say about the influence when one scholar becomes simply interested in the very same research areas as those investigated by the other scholar who aroused this interest through his writings. From this particular perspective, the thesis about the influence of Dargun on Malinowski cannot be so clearly rejected as it is justified in the case of strong understanding of notion of influence. Not going into portraying other possible "shades" of concept of influence, all this already proves that there still is a long way to reconstruct the entire picture of relationships between Dargun and Malinowski.

These considerations can be concluded with the following statement. Although the issue of Dargun's influence on Malinowski seems to be a real puzzle, which is very difficult to solve or maybe is even unsolvable, his work should be remembered, both in relation to Malinowski and independently of it. Undoubtedly, Dargun was a part of broad and very complex intellectual background from which Malinowski originated, but he was mainly a highly original, versatile and consistent scholar in his own right.

References

Anonymous Press Note. 1893a. Lotar Dargun. *Gazeta Lwowska* [*Lviv Newspaper*] 83(99) (May 2):4.

Anonymous Press Note. 1893b. Lotar Dargun. Wspomnienie pośmiertne [Lotar Dargun. Obituary]. *Przegląd Prawa i Administracyi* [*Law and Administration Review*] 18:417–421.

Dargun, L. 1879a. König Heinrich (VII). Beiträge und Ergänzungen [King Henry (VII). Contributions and additions]. *Forschungen zur Deutschen Geschichte* [*Research on German History*] 19:343–372.

Dargun, L. 1879b. Zum Problem des Ursprungs der Ehe [On the problem of the origin of marriage]. *Archiv für Anthropologie. Zeitschrift für Naturgeschichte und Urgeschichte des Menschen* [*Archive for Anthropology. Journal of Natural History and Prehistory of the People*] 11:125–131.

Dargun, L. 1880a. O pierwotnych formach własności [On the primary forms of property]. *Przegląd Sądowy i Administracyjny* [*Judicial and Administrative Review*] 5(14) (March 31):111–113 and 5(15) (April 8):121–123.

Dargun, L. 1880b. O początkach prawa spadkowego [On the beginnings of inheritance law]. *Przegląd Sądowy i Administracyjny* [*Judicial and Administrative Review*] 5(4) (January 21): 29–31.

Dargun, L. 1882a. O pokrewieństwie przez same tylko matki u dawnych Germanów [On the kinship by mothers alone among the old Germanic peoples]. *Rozprawy i sprawozdania z posiedzeń Wydziału Historyczno-Filozoficznego Akademii Umiejętności* [*Hearings and Reports of the Meetings of the Faculty of History and Philosophy of the Academy of Learning*] 15:248–350.

Dargun, L. 1882b. Prawo frankońskie i prawo światowe [Franconian law and global law]. *Przegląd Sądowy i Administracyjny* [*Judicial and Administrative Review*] 7(27) (July 5): 213–214 and 7(28) (July 12):221–223.

Dargun, L. 1883a. Mutterrecht und Raubehe und ihre Reste im germanischen Recht und Leben [Mother law and marriage by capture and their residues in Germanic law and life]. *Untersuchungen zur Deutschen Staats- und Rechtsgeschichte* [*Studies in History of German State and Law*] 16:I–VII, 1–161.

Dargun, L. 1883b. O zastosowaniu etnografii do historyi prawa [On the use of ethnography in history of law]. *Przewodnik naukowy i literacki* [*Scientific and Literary Guide*] 11, supplement to *Gazeta Lwowska* [*Lviv Newspaper*]:15–37.

Dargun, L. 1884a. Arbeitskapital und Normalerwerb [Working capital and normal acquisition]. *Zeitschrift für die gesamte Staatswissenschaft* [*Journal of the General Political Science*] 40(3-4):514–545.

Dargun, L. 1884b. O zabezpieczeniu robotników od wypadków [On the protection of workers from accidents]. *Przegląd Sądowy i Administracyjny* [*Judicial and Administrative Review*] 9(28) (July 9):219–221; 9(29) (July 16):229–231; 9(34) (August 20):273–274; 9(35) (August 27):279–280; 9(36) (September 3):287–289; 9(37) (September 10):296–297; and 9(38) (September 17):301–304.

Dargun, L. 1884c. Ursprung und Entwicklungs-Geschichte des Eigenthums [History of origin and development of property]. *Zeitschrift für vergleichende Rechtswissenschaft* [*Journal of Comparative Law*] 5:1–115.

Dargun, L. 1885. *Egoismus und Altruismus in der Nationalökonomie. Sociologische Studien. Erstes Heft* [*Egoism and altruism in national economy. Sociological studies, vol. 1*]. Leipzig: Verlag von Duncker & Humblot.

Dargun, L. 1887. Zur Methodik der sociologischen Rechtslehre [On the methodology of sociological theory of law]. *Archiv für öffentliches Recht* [*Archives of Public Law*] 2(3–4):542–566.

Dargun, L. 1888. O zabezpieczeniu robotników w teoryi i w najnowszem ustawodawstwie Austryi i Niemiec [On the protection of workers in the theory and the latest legislation of Austria and Germany]. *Przegląd Polski* [*Polish Review*] 23(2):136–166, 284–342.

Dargun, L. 1888/1891. O źródłach prawa miast polskich w wieku szesnastym. I. O źródłach przepisów karnych w dziełach Groickiego. II. O źródłach porządku sądowego spraw miejskich Prawa Magdeburskiego przez Bartłomieja Groickiego [On the sources of law of Polish cities in the sixteenth century. I. On the sources of penal provisions in the works of Groicki. II. On the sources of the court order in the municipal cases of Magdeburg law by Bartłomiej Groicki]. *Rozprawy i sprawozdania z posiedzeń Wydziału Historyczno-Filozoficznego Akademii Umiejętności* [*Hearings and Reports of the Meetings of the Faculty of History and Philosophy of the Academy of Learning*] 22 (1888):1–74 and 25 (1891):120–156.

Dargun, L. 1889. Die Reception der peinlichen Halsgerichtsordnung Kaiser Karls V. in Polen [Reception of penal code of Emperor Charles V in Poland]. *Zeitschrift der Savigny-Stiftung für Rechtsgeschichte. Germanistische Abtheilung* [*Journal of Savigny Foundation for History of Law. German Department*] 10:168–202.

Dargun, L. 1890. Altruismus [Altruism]. In *Handwörterbuch der Staatswissenschaften. Erster Band* [*Dictionary of political science, vol. 1*], ed. J. Conrad, L. Elster, W. Lexis, and E. Loening, 238–240. Jena: Verlag von Gustav Fischer.

Dargun, L. 1891. O rodzinie pierwotnej [On the primary family]. *Ateneum. Pismo naukowe i literackie* [*Athenaeum. Scientific and Literary Journal*] 4(2):240–266 and 4(3):471–515.

Dargun, L. 1892a. *Mutterrecht und Vaterrecht. Erste Hälfte. Die Grundlagen. Studien zum ältesten Familienrecht. Erster Teil, erste Hälfte* [*Mother law and father law. First half. The basics. Studies in the oldest family law. Part one, First half*]. Leipzig: Verlag von Duncker & Humblot.

Dargun, L. 1892b. O znaczeniu cywilizacyjnem wojny [On war's significance for civilization]. *Przegląd Polski* [*Polish Review*] 26(4):296–342.

Dargun, L. 1893. Iuris Ignorantia. *Czas* [*Time*] 46(23) (January 28):2a; 46(25) (January 31):2b and 46(26) (February 1):1–2.

Davies, P. 2010. *Myth, matriarchy and modernity. Johann Jakob Bachofen in German Culture, 1860-1945*. Berlin/New York: Walter de Gruyer.

Eller, C. 2011. *Gentlemen and Amazons. The myth of matriarchal prehistory, 1861-1900*. Berkeley: University of California Press.

Estreicher, S. 1895. Dargun Lothar v.: Mutterrecht und Vaterrecht (Studien zum ältesten Familienrecht). I Theil, erste Hälfte: Die Grundlagen. 1892 8° str. 115. *Kwartalnik Historyczny* [*Historical Quarterly*] 9:272–274.

Estreicher, S. 1902. Początki prawa umownego [The beginnings of contract law]. *Rozprawy Akademii Umiejętności. Wydział Historyczno-Filozoficzny. Serya II* [*Hearings of the Academy of Learning. Faculty of History and Philosophy. Second Series*] 16:228–399.

Jaworski, W.L. 1893. Lotar Dargun. *Przegląd Prawa i Administracyi* [*Law and Administration Review*] 18:497–513, 569–583.

K., E. 1893. Lotar Dargun. *Gazeta Sądowa Warszawska* [*Warsaw Judicial Newspaper*] 21(18) (May 1):342–343.

Kubica, G. 1986. Bronisław Malinowski's years in Poland. *JASO (Journal of the Anthropological Society of Oxford)* 17(2):140–154.

Malinowski, B. 1913. *The family among Australian aborigines. A sociological study*. London: University of London Press.

Malinowski, B. 1930. Kinship. *Man* 30(February):19–29.

Malinowski, B. 1962. Marriage. In *Sex, culture and myth*, B Malinowski, 3–35. New York: Harcourt, Brace & World. Originally published: 1929. In *Encyclopaedia Britannica*, 14th edn, vol. 14:940–950.

Malinowski, B. 1993. The sociology of the family. In *The early writings of Bronisław Malinowski*, ed. R.J. Thornton and P. Skalník (trans: L. Krzyżanowski), 247–268. Cambridge: Cambridge University Press. Originally published: 1914. Soziologie der Familie. *Die Geisteswissenschaften* 1(32):883–886; 1(33):911–914 and 1(39):1080–1082.

Paluch, A.K. 1988. Introduction: Bronisław Malinowski and Cracow anthropology. In *Malinowski between two worlds. The Polish roots of an anthropological tradition*, ed. R. Ellen, E. Gellner, G. Kubica, and J. Mucha, 1–11. Cambridge: Cambridge University Press.

Patkaniowski, M. 1964a. *Dzieje Wydziału Prawa Uniwersytetu Jagiellońskiego od reformy kołłątajowskiej do końca XIX stulecia* [*History of the Faculty of Law at the Jagiellonian University since Hugo Kołłątaj's reform until the end of the nineteenth century*]. Kraków: Nakładem Uniwersytetu Jagiellońskiego.

Patkaniowski, M. 1964b. Od prawa niemieckiego do powszechnej historii prawa. Lotar Dargun (1853-1893) – Stanisław Estreicher (1869-1939) [From German law to the general history of law. Lotar Dargun (1853-1893) – Stanisław Estreicher (1869-1939)]. In *Studia z dziejów Wydziału Prawa Uniwersytetu Jagiellońskiego* [*Studies in the history of the Faculty of Law at the Jagiellonian University*], ed. M. Patkaniowski, 223–239. Kraków: Nakładem Uniwersytetu Jagiellońskiego.

Pol, K. 2011. Lotar Dargun (1853-1893). In *Poczet prawników polskich XIX-XX w.* [*Gallery of Polish lawyers from the XIX-XX century*], Second Edition, K. Pol, 473–478. Warszawa: Wydawnictwo C.H. Beck.

Posner, S. 1893a. Lotar Dargun (Wspomnienie pozgonne) [Lotar Dargun (Obituary)]. *Prawda. Tygodnik polityczny, społeczny i literacki* [*Truth. Political, social and literary weekly*] 13(32) (August 12):374–376.

Posner, S. 1893b. Lotar Dargun i jego zasługi w dziedzinie prawa porównawczego [Lotar Dargun and his contributions in the field of comparative law]. *Gazeta Sądowa Warszawska* [*Warsaw Judicial Newspaper*] 21(34) (August 21):585–593 and 21(35) (August 28):601–608.

Post, A.H. 1891. Ethnological jurisprudence (trans: T.J. McCormack). *The Monist* 2(1): 31–40.

Potkański, K. 1893. Naukowa działalność Lotara Darguna [Scientific activities of Lotar Dargun]. *Przegląd Polski* [*Polish Review*] 28(2):122–164.

Schott, R. 1982. Main trends in German ethnological jurisprudence and legal ethnology. *Journal of Legal Pluralism* 20:37–68.

Smith, M. 1893. Studien zum Aeltesten Familienrecht. Erster Teil: Mutterrecht und Vaterrecht. Erste Hälfte: Die Grundlagen. Von Dr. LOTHAR VON DARGUN, Professor an der Universität Krakau. Leipzig, Duncker & Humblot, 1892.–8vo, 155 pp. *Political Science Quarterly* 8(3): 572–575.

Stępień, M. 2014. Bronisława Malinowskiego potyczki z prawem (prymitywnym) [Bronisław Malinowski's skirmishes with the (primitive) law]. In *Wielowymiarowość prawa* [*Multidimensionality of law*], ed. J. Czapska, M. Dudek, and M. Stępień, 403–426. Toruń: Wydawnictwo Adam Marszałek.

Thornton, R., and P. Skalník. 1993. Introduction: Malinowski's reading, writing, 1904-1914. In *The early writings of Bronisław Malinowski*, ed. R.J. Thornton and P. Skalník (trans: L. Krzyżanowski), 1–64. Cambridge: Cambridge University Press.

Wagner-Hasel, B. 2003. Egoistic exchange and altruistic gift. On the roots of Marcel Mauss's theory of the gift. In *Negotiating the gift. Pre-modern figurations of exchange*, ed. G. Algazi, V. Groebner, and B. Jussen, 141–171. Göttingen: Vandenhoeck & Ruprecht.

Żukowski, P.M. 2014. *Profesorowie Wydziału Prawa Uniwersytetu Jagiellońskiego. Tom II. 1780-2012* [*Professors of the Faculty of Law at the Jagiellonian University, vol. II. 1780–2012*], ed. D. Malec. Kraków: Wydawnictwo Uniwersytetu Jagiellońskiego.

Chapter 2
Stanisław Estreicher: The Forgotten Master of Bronislaw Malinowski

Krzysztof Pałecki

2.1 The Intellectual Inspirations of Malinowski

The quest for scientific inspiration has, apart from satisfying the curiosity of the kind of "where did he take it from?", at least two more values. Above all, it allows for a better understanding of a given scientific work, not only of its assumptions but also of its final solutions. Additionally, it enables a proper assessment of the originality of the thought, as well as the evaluation of the contribution into the existing state of knowledge made by a scientist. In the case of Bronislaw Malinowski, there can be distinguished another specific reason for the search of his scientific roots—the reason resulting from his complex biography. Usually, it proves relatively easy to identify both persons, as well as works that exerted a significant influence on the manner of conducting research work and results obtained by a scientist. The answer to the question about his intellectual—and, possibly, personal—master usually does not pose a problem for historians. Bronislaw Malinowski, however, "appeared" on the scene of the world science from "out of nowhere", from the remote intellectual corners of then "eastern Europe", barely known in the West. He came from the society whose great past had already been—willingly and partly intentionally—long forgotten and which was not able to present its scientific achievements on the international scene of knowledge as a politically independent state. It was in such specific historical conditions of the early twentieth century that Bronislaw Malinowski embarked on his scientific career, entering the circles of the British social science, which, although still leading in many fields, was forced to face the growing "global" competition from the United States. In the years 1910–1913, Malinowski was still merely one of many "exotic" students of the London School of Economics. Already at that time,

K. Pałecki (✉)
Department of Sociology of Law, Jagiellonian University, Krakow, Poland
e-mail: krzysztof.palecki@uj.edu.pl

M. Stępień (ed.), *Bronislaw Malinowski's Concept of Law*,
DOI 10.1007/978-3-319-42025-7_2

however, his opinions frequently met with interest from the narrow circle of his peers. It was only after 1927, upon his appointment to the Chair of Anthropology as a professor of the London University, that he entered the pedestal of the "world" science. A significant part of his further scientific achievements was made under the brand of this excellent "company": as a British professor, the author of the "British ethnology of culture" or "British field researcher", etc. Years later, while being introduced to the *honoris causa* degree at the Harvard University (1936), he was thus titled in the laudation, whereas his "Polish roots" were mentioned merely out of politeness. However, on his arrival to London, the young Malinowski had already boasted the excellent PhD thesis on philosophy, titled *On the Economy of Thinking*, defended at the Jagiellonian University. Moreover, for many years he had been an active participant in the intellectual discourse in one of the finest scientific, artistic and political circles, whose representatives received their education at the universities of Vienna, Paris, Berlin, Heidelberg and Saint Petersburg, and also, by participating in research and lectures, exerted a significant "return" influence on the shape of knowledge offered by those centers.

Therefore, it seems justifiable to pose a question about "pre-British" scientific inspirations of Bronislaw Malinowski, the question about the roots, the "origin" of his scientific "approach", his theoretical and empirical assumptions and the world of his problems, concepts and generalizations. To put the task posed in this paper simply: we want to show how the influence of only one man, Stanisław Estreicher (1869–1939), could shape the earliest knowledge of the new entrant to science, student, graduate and young doctor of the Jagiellonian University, Bronislaw Malinowski. In this paper we like to pay attention to Stanisław Estreicher's earlier merits into Malinowski, not exposed before. This is a story of the influence of the man whom the latter shall always consider as his master, "his professor" and—with time—his friend. Malinowski mentioned in the preface of a book of one of his pupils, Felix Gross: "I have also been associated with our ancient University of Cracow [i.e. Jagiellonian University—ed. K.P.]. I also, like Dr Gross, have been inspired in my work the teachings and personal interests of Professor Stanislaw Estreicher. I have also started to primitive societies in the library, and was only later' able to go out into the field" (1936b, p. xiii). Therefore, we shall unveil the most essential concepts of Stanisław Estreicher, frequently being common truths of his times and, even more, of his intellectual environment. The concepts which would later appear in the works by Bronislaw Malinowski, often in new editions or as characteristic "reference points" in polemics he entered into. However, regardless of whether later he remained loyal to them or whether he criticized them, even a cursory review easily reveals the fact that they were permanently "rooted" in the intellectual consciousness of Malinowski, in his axiology and the way he perceived the world. Upon a closer look, "the scholar from nowhere" proves to be a newcomer from a specific academic *milieu*, boasting an interesting scientific pedigree, a scientist who had not received the well-deserved extensive publicity only because of unfavorable circumstances.

As for the objective scope of the opinion presented above, we shall concentrate mainly on the problem of the "primitive law", or, to be more precise, the law of pre-state societies ("savage", "non-civilized", "primitive" ones, etc.). Already at the beginning, it seems characteristic that to Bronislaw Malinowski, the problem of the "primitive law" was far more important and complex than to the majority of his contemporary anthropologists, who only sporadically—usually in discussions on customs and religions of "the primitive"—brought up this question. Of them, only some and only much later followed his tracks in this field (Znamierowski 2001, p. ix). We shall not further discuss this question, but we seem justified to assume that such an intensive interest in the origins of law shown by Malinowski (a philosopher by education and, initially, a researcher on epistemological problems), was a consequence of his contacts with the person and teachings of Stanislaw Estreicher, who, in addition to his numerous qualifications and public functions, made primarily an eminent historian of law.

It was on his lectures on the beginnings of law (Franconian, German, Polish and others) that Malinowski, at that time still a student of philosophy, could for the first time hear about the concept of the evolution of law (Patkaniowski 1964, p. 233). In the "*Program*" (*An Outline*) of those lectures (preserved in the Central Archives of Historical Records in Warsaw—46u-F5, fasc.14), made soon after (as already in 1894) the popularization of the groundbreaking *Ancient Law* by Sir Henry Sumner Maine in the continental science of law, Estreicher thoroughly explained the necessity for examining "the reasons behind creation, flourishing and death of legal institutions" (Patkaniowski 1964, p. 229). In the development to this concept, in the "*Program*" (*An Outline*) there appear the problems of "primitive" land possession, "primitive" principles of inheritance, "primitive" family relationships, bases of law, the relationship to "witchcraft" and others, whose clear traces can later be found in the research and numerous works by Bronislaw Malinowski. Undoubtedly, it must have been from this very source that Malinowski learned about the meanders of universal evolutionism by Herbert Spencer and social evolutionism by August Comte and Emil Durkheim, as well as about pioneering ethnographic works by Levis H. Morgan, Franz Boas, the discourse on the origins of the "German" law led among representatives of the so-called German Historical School (Karl von Savigny, Georg Puchta, Otto Gierke, Rudolf von Ihering and others) and, conceivably, about many other fields and researchers. Also, it was Estreicher who later submitted the concepts by Karl von Savigny and Rudolf von Ihering to severe criticism, well-known in the circles of lawyers. The first one was criticized for explaining the similarities between customs by the German mystic "*Volkgeist*", while Ihering for "ascribing to primitive peoples the opinions borrowed from our stock of thoughts" (Estreicher 1901, pp. 4, 10 and others). He was also the first one to specify the concept of "primitive people", present in works of conceivably all coryphées of anthropology of culture (and law), by determining empirical criteria qualifying to designates of this term (Estreicher 1901, pp. 25 and next).

2.2 The Master Turned Friend

If, as we are justified to think, that was the case, we should spend a while analyzing the character of this specific relationship connecting Stanisław Estreicher and Bronislaw Malinowski. What conceals under this slightly enigmatic statement that the former was the master to the latter, the statement to which we are trying to convince a reader? Surely, we can formulate such a conclusion with a pretty specific understanding of performing the profession of a scientist. We are of the opinion that in sciences on society the absolute originality of basic assumptions formulated in the "pure" form, "unspoiled" by borrowings from other scientists simply does not exist. We also think that a thorough source review of the biography of a given researcher almost always reveals his "masters" (or a "master"). The profession of a scientist shares a lot with crafts; one develops his own manner of performing the job in the process of acquiring knowledge from his masters. Therefore, also scientists have their own "masters" who shaped them indirectly—exclusively by their works, without any form of personal contact, often being simply impossible. Many a time, however, we can find examples of masters influencing their "disciples" directly, by personal contact. Such an influence is equal or even stronger than the indirect one. To simplify, depending on what ultimately proves to be more essential for the work of a scientist, we can distinguish "masters through works" and "masters through personality". In the relationship "master—disciple" here discussed, Stanisław Estreicher's seems to appear in the double role, in the both kinds of mentorship at different times. During the studies of Bronislaw Malinowski in Kraków, it was Estreicher's lectures, papers and works that gradually shaped, more or less consciously, the later "intellectual basis" of the young researcher. With time, however, despite the age difference (15 years), the former appeared to the latter as not only an ideal of a scientist and his intellectual authority, but also an invaluable advisor, also in personal affairs, finally to become his friend. In the so-called *Zbiory Estreicherowskie* (*Estreicherian Collection*) of the Kraków Society of Friends of Fine Arts—the society of which Stanisław Estreicher's son, Karol (called "junior") for many years was the President—there have preserved letters and postcards written by Malinowski on his travels, addressed to his "My Dear Stanisław" and even "Beloved Stanisław", showing the degree of their familiarity. We are of the opinion that this complex process of "mentorship" cannot be separated from the biography of the "master" himself, in its beginnings bearing striking resemblance to the biography of his "disciple".

2.3 Professional Background of Stanisław Estreicher

Stanisław Estreicher, similarly to Malinowski, was born in the highly renowned family of professors of the Jagiellonian University, in the year 1869. His grandfather, Alojzy Rafał Estreicher (1786–1852) was a professor and the rector of this university, a distinguished botanist and the founder of one of the first botanical gardens in Europe (operating in unchanged scientific foundations until today). His grandfather, Karol Estreicher (called "senior", 1827–1908), gained fame as a historian of Polish literature and, for years, as the honored director of the Jagiellonian University Library. Stanisław, just like his brother Tadeusz, a professor of chemistry, undertook studies at the Jagiellonian University, although at the Faculty of Law. However, from the very beginning, his interests significantly departed from the majority of lectures on law, usually being narrowly dogmatic. The only exception made the lectures by professor Lotar Dargun, who, being not only a lawyer, but primarily an eminent humanist and historian (see Chap. 1), excited in Stanisław Estreicher an enthusiastic interest with his research on the "primitive law" and the beginnings of the state system, as well as with his legal-comparative, ethnographic and sociological knowledge. Stanislaw Estreicher soon began to consider him as his master, and, in a relatively short time (after Dargun's death in 1893), became his successor as the Head of Department of History of the State and German law (Patkaniowski 1964, pp. 232 and next). He also felt obliged to continue his master's research on law, however, in the scope far exceeding—both temporally and horizontally—the history of German and Polish law, by applying comparative methods and knowledge from the fields of ethnology (ethnography), political science and sociology. Those methods, as to their rules borrowed from Lotar Dargun and representatives of the so-called Kraków historical school (especially Michał Bobrzyński and Bolesław Ulanowski), were successfully applied by Estreicher in the research on the problems of the origins of the family law, ownership law, law of political systems, and, especially, in the most valued research on the beginnings of the contractual law. Michał Patkaniowski thus wrote about them: "written 60 years ago, the work of immense erudition, also today can serve as the ideal of an objective scientific method" (Patkaniowski 1964, p. 233).

They assured him the position of a professor and the recognition which soon translated into the positions of the Dean of the Faculty of Law of the Jagiellonian University (1911/2, 1918/9, 1926/7), the Rector of this university (1919–1921) and the Vice-rector (1921–1922). Worth mentioning here is his cycle of works devoted to the "ancient law", including the Code of Hammurabi, almost immediately after its discovery in 1901 in Suza. Already in 1905 there appeared its elaboration by Estreicher: "*The Code of Hammurabi*", and, subsequently, in 1931: "*The Oldest Codes of Law in the World*", "*Legal Culture of Western Asia in the Second Thousand before Christ*", and others. All of the works characterized with an unusual—as for the then condition of historical legal sciences—ethnographic knowledge and the argumentation disciplined by clearly expressed research assumptions. Certainly, such a strong interest in the Code of Hammurabi shown by Stanisław Estreicher stemmed also, or perhaps chiefly, from the fact that he considered it to be one of the crucial proofs for the evolutionary character of cultural phenomena, including the system of law, being essential to Estreicher. His epistemic convictions, as well as his opinions on nature of social reality, and, especially, normative world, Stanisław Estreicher formulated relatively early, mainly under the influence of readings of "first sociologists"—August Comte,

Herbert Spencer, Emil Durkheim, which found its full reflection in the above-cited "*Beginnings of Contractual Law*" (1901). The reasons for which we shall try to outline only some of these opinions are two. The first one is connected with the length limitations; tracing back all the literal similarities in the formulations and terminology of Estreicher ("master") and Malinowski ("disciple") far exceeds, because of the volume of their scientific work, the possibilities and the size of this paper. The other one is of substantive nature. The "relationship" between their thoughts was not always expressed directly—in the use of the same language, the same terminology. This would be simply impossible, as Estreicher used linguistic forms still belonging to the nineteenth century (not only in Polish texts, but also in e.g. German ones). Malinowski, a modernist by conviction and because of his professional contacts, used a much modern form of the Polish language, contemporary to him, later to write only in English (and American English). Hence, all that is common for their scientific work is observable only on the level of basic assumptions adopted by both of them. However, even here one must be careful for, with time, the "late Malinowski" changed, filled and gave many generalizations made by the "young Malinowski" a more conditional mode, whereas Stanisław Estreicher specialized in general theses. Nevertheless, from the context, quoted factual examples, authorial explanations, the manner and the selection of arguments, in many crucial questions the originality of which is ascribed only to Malinowski, a more primordial source can easily be indicated. Obviously, this "source" was not only of the authorship by Stanisław Estreicher, who is intentionally given such extensive exposure, on the basis of *licentia discutionis,* as if he had been the only one. However, the role of Malinowski's "master" certainly refers also to other scientists, both previous ones and his contemporary ones. It also refers to those eminent scientists from whom Stanisław Estreicher himself derived his knowledge and patterns of scientific activity, including Lotar Dargun, and, as it turns out, especially from Leon Petrażycki (Kurczewski 2012, pp. 64 and next). While taking the first step in that direction and leaving the decision on the relevance of the above conviction to a reader, let us try to trace back the main assumptions of the scientific activity conducted by Stanisław Estreicher.

2.4 Naturalistic Assumptions

Naturalism, often confused with organicism, was undoubtedly the essential ontological assumption of Stanisław Estreicher (1901, pp. 11–12), the assumption which he even did not try to conceal. We dare to think that it is still present in convictions expressed by a larger part of the environment of anthropologists of culture. Understood as the rejection of the unique character of social processes and the adoption as necessary of the number of relationships between "science and culture", "somatics and personality", etc.—the relationships whose "suspension" (omission) has the character exclusively analytical (i.e. being a procedure merely organizing the course of deliberations or experiments), to many contemporary anthropologists, sociologists, empirically-oriented researchers of law and others makes the foundation for the legitimization of applying natural methods and techniques of research. Alfred L. Kroeber thus comments on this problem: "It seems to me essential to recognize culture as a 'level' or 'order' of natural phenomena; the level characterized with specific organization (...). The emergence of phenomena of life from the non-organic being is conceivably the earliest and the most essential diversification of such orders or levels" (Kroeber 2009, p. 280). It should be mentioned that this "synergistic" view, fully shared, although differently stylized, by both Stanisław Estreicher and Bronislaw Malinowski, does not lead Kroeber to reducionistic conclusions, but to methodological postulates: the research on "manifestations of life also in a biological way" (similarly Malinowski 2001, p. 18).

The consequence of the naturalistic assumption was the reluctance or even sharp criticism expressed by Stanisław Estreicher against a number of fashionable, contemporary to him conceptualizations explaining social life. He claimed that basic legal institutions were established neither "out of wisdom of a legislator" (anti-rationalism), nor "out of will of a ruler" (against creative voluntarism). Nor they are the result of a certain form of agreement (contract) made between the "interested parties" (against concepts of social contract). They cannot also be the consequence of the "will of people", the "spirit of nation", "common human psychics", etc. (against holistic psychologism). While rejecting the concepts of the "universal, timeless psychics", which would allegedly explain the existence of similarities between normative regulations (including legal ones) in societies remote geographically, historically and civilizationally, Estreicher claimed: "Today, reasoning about motives of acting and thinking of a primitive man according to the data collected from our daily life runs contrary to the whole direction of new ethnographic and historical research" (Estreicher 1901, p. 12). Here it seems worth paying attention to the use of the term "motives of conduct", derived from the terminology of Leon Petrażycki (1925). Estreicher frequently pointed out the error of the "universal psychologism", while comparing different legal regulations (Estreicher 1901, p. 12). For instance he writes: "The conviction that the primitive man has, similarly to us today, economic carefulness, that in his actions and organizations he follows the same common sense as the people of the late 19th century (...) is the common defect of numerous historical constructions, referring to organizations from the more remote past (...)". Further below he states: "(...) there is a total opposition of motives of conduct and generally the whole psychology between us and the peoples on the lowest level of civilization" (Estreicher 1901, p. 13). Estreicher in this question refers also to scientific achievements: "After 1880 there appeared studies on primitive peoples and their result was in the first place the discovery of the psychology of the man of nature being completely different from the psychological system of the man of civilization" (1901, p. 13). The very same error is later found in argumentations of Malinowski, however, in reference to not only law, but also other "fragments of culture".

2.5 The Evolutionism of Stanislaw Estreicher

The consequence of adopting naturalistic ontology by Stanisław Estreicher was his specific evolutionism. At its basis we can easily notice the "mixture" of concepts by Comte, Spencer and Durkheim, although devoid of their optimistic progresivistic convictions and with the clear "echo" of Morgan's classification of history and references to the theory of conquest (Estreicher 1901, p. 28). The evolution of societies consists in developing, "more and more extensive and diversified social organizations (. . .), the destination of which is to absorb a separate social life of smaller groups, as the result of the development of one and the same original group". Such "'unification' only rarely is voluntary, resulting from common needs of peaceful or war character. More frequently, this impulse to the unification results from violence and conquest by a certain group aimed against several other neighboring, hence similarly civilized, groups. (. . .) The collapsing division into groups (. . .) is replaced with a far more horizontal division into certain asset classes, unified politically and professionally. There emerge differences in the way of life, customs, needs and means leading to their fulfillment" (Estreicher 1901, pp. 46–47). Moreover, "the more we step back into the most ancient depths of history, the smaller the variety of life conditions, racial character, views on the world (. . .) and the larger the similarity of concepts and organizations of peoples being completely strange to one another. In the embryonic state of societies, the similarities are as much striking as physiological similarities in the animal world in that state" (Estreicher 1901, p. 14).

Apart from evolutionary processes of the quantitative growth of primitive collectivities of people (groups, "closer and more extensive" groups, as he later defined them), processes of "absorption" of one group by another and their assimilation, processes of labor division and diversification of structures, the emergence of seeds of the political system described by Estreicher, there are also other specific forms of the progressing evolution worth mentioning. On the one hand, there appears a group, collective adaptation to changing needs and living conditions, while, on the other hand, there appears the process of "liberating an individual" from the bonds of collective solidarity, the process allowing for the individualization of activities, gradual liberation from the ways of life identical to everyone leading to individual empowerment, as we describe it today. Let us observe that such a concept is present practically in the whole work of Bronislaw Malinowski, being especially visible in his deliberations upon the "legal" foundations of mutual obligations of individual members of a tribe.

For Stanisław Estreicher, nothing that appears in the evolutionary process of society is accidental or redundant. He teaches that to convince oneself about this fact one should place any object of culture in a historically proper context of conditions from whose appearance and for which the given element emerged and functions. This obviously refers also to law: "As no concept and no legal regulation appears accidentally, but each of them is, sometimes even unconsciously, the creation of certain general needs and aspirations (. . .)" (Estreicher 1901, p. 23). It is difficult not to agree that these words would later echo in the later functional concepts of Bronislaw Malinowski, dominated by, at least until the appearance of the concept of dysfunction formulated by Robert Merton, the principle of total pragmatism (theological necessity) of all institutions existing in a given social system. In his "*Anthropology*", Malinowski states: "(...) in each type of society, every custom, material object, idea and belief (...) serves a certain purpose, being a necessary part of the functioning whole" (Malinowski 1936a, p. 132). Pragmatism, as one of the main adopted assumptions, obliges Stanisław Estreicher, by careful examination of any "social organization" (normative regulation) from the "distant past", to each time pose the same basic question: what is its purpose? And the answer to it should be reduced to indicating a specific, important and over individual need for the fulfillment of which this "organization" is supposed to be a more or less effective instrument.

At the basis of such an approach there lies Estreicher's conviction about the one-way direction of evolution of the whole humanity, resulting from the identity of basic human needs, needs which must, to a certain degree, be satisfied by evolutionary changes (in the first place food, safety, shelter and reproduction). Needless to say, Malinowski shared the very same conviction as evidenced, for example, in the following statement: "The functional ethnological theory conceives culture as the instrumental reality. The most essential thing, as far as culture is concerned, is that it allows a man to satisfy his basic needs, i.e. the needs for safety, protection from weather and the surrounding environment, as well as his procreative needs" (Malinowski 2001, p. 17). This conviction is complemented by Estreicher while deliberating upon and accepting the advantages of the research conducted by applying the comparative method—the problem to be discussed later—with the following statements: "as this [method—ed. K.P.] recognizes the uniformity of the whole immensity of peoples in the world and the resulting identity of cultural development (...) the comparative direction, under which the whole latest science of history of law is developing and which is also beginning, although not that fast, to exert a significant influence on other fields of the history of human culture, is obviously based upon the conviction that the whole humanity makes the uniform whole whose individual parts cover at different pace the same paths of development" (Estreicher 1901, p. 13). This also explains his more specific approach to the problem of separation of the "German culture" (in fact—the originality of customs in pre-state German tribes): "it [the comparative method—ed. K.P.] rejects the hypothesis that German peoples could produce tools essentially different from those produced by other peoples and develop them in a way different from the development met elsewhere" (Estreicher 1901, p. 15).

The collective (group, tribal) reaction to the need for satisfying basic universal needs, the reaction being not necessarily conscious and even less necessarily intentionally led, is a proper method of organizing a given community, and—what it inherently involves—formulating rules of conduct (customs, religions, law)—not necessarily being "copies" of those existing elsewhere (Estreicher 1901, p. 13). A separate attention should be paid to the frequently used by Stanisław Estrecher term "organization" ("legal organization"), sometimes replaced by "legal institution" (Estreicher 1901, p. 23). To him, it does not mean merely a normative regulation, but also all that is connected with the practice of its application and sanctioning. The well-known sociological concept of the "institution" by Bronislaw Malinowski, not only being a "set of legal regulations", but comprising "the group of people united in common task (…), disposing common technical tools and governed by a certain set of rules", is exactly the same concept, but expressed in a different term (see: Malinowski 2001, pp. 19–20).

2.6 The Impact of Cracow's Historians

As already mentioned, the methodological assumptions and concepts adopted by Stanisław Estreicher are primarily the reflection of more common views shared by representatives of the so-called Kraków historical school, the more eminent of whom were his academic teachers (and undoubtedly his "masters", e.g. Michał Bobrzyński, Bolesław Ulanowski, Stanisław Tarnowski). The "school" postulated the methodical research work, based on reliable, authentic and multisource empirical data, comparatistics, diachronic approach and the recreation of the original historic context of examined events and other "products of culture" (Estreicher 1936, p. 16). Estreicher, faithful to these principles, ironically criticized works of some researchers of history, especially representatives of the doctrine of the law of nature, describing their "research" as "accidental and antiquarian work" (Estreicher 1901, p. 3). An additional and clear influence on his methodological convictions had also sociological works of the "first positivism", especially those by August Comte (Estreicher 1901, p. 12). It was from him that Estreicher "borrowed" the distrust to deduction from abstract theorems, the conviction about the value of direct observation, inductive procedures, the historiosophical search for explaining "the present from the past" and, above all, the advantages of the comparative method as: "the best way of learning culture and psychics of primitive peoples" (Estreicher 1901, p. 12). In reference to explaining a given "institution of law' from its past, it is worth quoting the following view expressed by Estrecher: "When we want to explain a given institution of law, we must turn back to the times when it is in the process of shaping, when it appears aggressively, gaining the field for development and displacing previous concepts and organizations" (Estreicher 1901, p. 24). Comparative operations in his understanding should comprise the whole material and non-material culture, especially normative regulations, including the law of individual "primitive peoples".

Moreover, one should not neglect comparatistics, which uses the knowledge on cultures of these "prehistoric peoples" comparing it with the features of cultures in contemporary societies (cultures of "civilized peoples"). The conviction that such comparisons are explanatorily valuable and even necessary was shared by both of the scientists. Malinowski wrote: "The translation of principles of primitive customary law into the contemporary one (…) is not only possible, but it has already been successfully made in both practice as well as in theory. (…) I am of the opinion that in this aspect there is no essential lack of continuity between our society and the society of primitive peoples" (Malinowski 2001, pp. 16–17).

Before returning to the comparative method in the approach of Estreicher, it is necessary to notice, again from the striking similarity of these views to the formulations of Bronislaw Malinowski, the constantly repeating Estreicher's objection against the adoption of deductive, empirically not verifiable generalizations and assumption, prejudging the direction and results of performed explanations (e.g. by classicists of the German school of history of law, supporters of various kinds of psychologism, as well as followers of dialectical materialism, and others). As he wrote: "It is the time when the turn against speculations (...) and towards connecting mental phenomena with material phenomena is very strong in science" (Estreicher 1901, p. 12).

2.7 Comparatistic Approach

For Stanisław Estreicher, the application of the comparative method, both synchronically and diachronically, was intended to be a specific panaceum for numerous defects of not only the research on law, but also on culture tout court, on "social life in its whole". He specifically meant the sanation of opportunistic habits of researchers (including historians of law and ethnologists), consisting in using the first available source materials, limited temporally, territorially and essentially, and poorly confirmed in empirical research. He also had strong reservations as to the common ignoring of sociological, psychological, economic and political research and theories in the process of explaining legal texts (and—more generally, normative regulations). Thus, for example, he wrote while leveling his criticism against the condition of the research on the "law of primitive peoples": "As for legal development, one must find new sources or a new method if the previously known sources and the old method do not provide a sufficient basis for recreating the starting point for legal evolution (...). In the context of the already mentioned comments, the comparative method can serve, in a large part, as the most suitable way leading to learning about legal relationships of those [i.e. "primitive"—ed. K. P.] societies (...)" (Estreicher 1901, pp. 14, 24). Earlier, in his introductory comments to the "*Beginnings of Contractual Law*" Estreicher wrote: "Such a method [i.e. free from the defects of previously applied methods—ed. K. P.] in today's state of knowledge is undoubtedly the comparative method, and such sources for learning about the legal relationships of European peoples from the pre-historic epoch is news on other—today's or past—ancient peoples". Stanisław Estreicher boasted an exceptional "methodological awareness", and therefore he warned those researchers who applied comparative techniques against their potential dangers: "The comparative method—he wrote—as far as the relationships of upper stages of civilization are concerned, undoubtedly requires great reservations and carefulness, especially because all too often it is used recklessly and imprecisely: often analogies and homologies in the development of certain social organizations are mixed and treated equally, as identical phenomena. The similarity resulting from the reception of a certain organization is not distinguished from the similarity resulting from the racial relationship of two societies (...)". However, he soon adds: "But, as for the comparative method applied in the research on primitive peoples, in today's condition of science it is far more elaborated and it should replace any speculations in retracing pre-historic social relationships" (Estreicher 1901, pp. 14–15).

For those doubting in epistemological relationship between Malinowski and Estreicher,—separated, admittedly, by the over twenty-year caesura of the passing time—I shall quote a fragment from the former, glorifying ethnographical work of the "field worker", as he would often call himself: "Instead of erecting immense constructions based on the reconstruction—either evolutionary or diffusionistic—it seemed better to turn onto the path of the analysis of today's reality of individual cultures. The resulting comparative calculations have led us to the discovery of laws of cultural development and to definitions of essential concepts lying at the basis of each single cultural reality" (Malinowski 2001, p. 4).

2.8 The Essential Approximations

Here we touch upon yet another, not accidental—as we are justified to think—and being of vital cognitive importance, similarity in conceiving the examined material appearing between the two scientists. Estreicher, exactly as later Malinowski, coped with the dilemma of similarities appearing in different, temporally and territorially separated cultures, especially the similarities between "social organizations", or—in Malinowski's terminology—"institutions". The similarities which by no means could be explained by some "exchange" or contacts between societies in which those similarities were observed. Further, at the same time, both scientists were fascinated by the wealth of completely different normative regulations (including the legal ones), organizational solutions, material objects, images, values and views discovered successively by "field" researchers in communities (tribes) maintaining close (relatively close) neighborly contacts. This triggered significant complications, as both scientists shared the conviction about universal "general laws governing processes (...) shaping the reality of culture" existing in social reality, whose discovery: "is and shall be the scientific task of ethnology" (Malinowski 2001, p. 5).

Stanisław Estreicher "managed" to find the solution to this dilemma (of difficult to explain convergences and, equally difficult in this aspect, "unexplainable" cultural varieties) in a very modern, Weberian one could say, way. It seems best to quote his words: "(...) it is not consistent with the basis of the comparative direction to construct a scheme of development different for each of societies; assumedly, the scheme achieved for one nation can also be applied in the understanding of development (...) of other nations. Naturally, we speak here only about the scheme: the details of development shall always be different" (Estreicher 1901,

p. 25). Estreicher's "scheme", constructed as the generalization of repetitive, "essential" similarities, bears a striking resemblance to the later concept of "ideal models" formulated by Max Weber, and commonly known to methodologists of social research.

Estreicher's assertions made in the context of research on history of contractual law were later repeated by Malinowski—with clearly visible analogy—in his deliberations upon the problem of the "existence of primitive law", reserving that the argument on its existence—which he adopted as obvious—as well as its possible negation cannot consist in pointing out a literal similarity or, on the contrary, in non-agreeable dissimilarity between the contents of pre-historic regulations and contemporary laws, but in empirical statement of the fact of appearing in all: "societies differentiated (temporally or culturally)—other organs of judgments (. . .), the punishing hand of justice, (. . .) police, a secret association or hired killers who execute the verdict of law" (Malinowski 2001, pp. 46–47).

If, as we are trying to prove, between Stanisław Estreicher and Bronislaw Malinowski there truly existed—in a definable extent—the relationship "master-disciple", then certainly, as it has already been proven, it cannot and should not be justified either by literal similarities of their terminology or the identical form of their theorems. One should rather refer to the clear relevance of general research assumptions they adopted and the closeness of concrete substantive solutions. What is also important is the similar, sometimes even identical, way in which they conceived the object of research. Having adopted such argumentation, it is worth paying attention to another, again rather not accidental, and conceivably—the most essential, analogy appearing in works by the two scientists. Let us call this analogy, being often neglected, normative essentialism. We could also, indicating adequate fragments of works of the two researchers, coin the term of "cultural essentialism", which would be reduced to the conviction that the shape of the whole culture of any given society is the result of reactive-adaptive processes, caused by changing conditions of satisfying needs ("basic derivatives"), and not intended, planned, consciously implemented innovations of secondary importance. In this sense for both of them culture is primarily a natural and not volitional creation. Therefore, it is governed by "natural", "objective" and "common" laws, the "discovery" of which is the task of researchers examining culture. Reducing objectively "normative essentialism" to law, which—as Malinowski puts it—"is the essential pre-requisite of all cultural processes" (Malinowski 2001, p. 19) it seems justified to introduce yet another term of "legal essentialism". The view described under this term is again shared by both Malinowski and Estreicher. From different fragments of their works, in the case of Estreicher referring mainly, although not exclusively, to the process of shaping of contractual law, whereas in the case of Malinowski—mainly to (individual) ownership law and family relationships, there emerges a strong conviction that law, and—analogically—all the remaining kinds of normative regulations, are based, regardless of time and place of their appearance, on one basic principle, one "imperative" or "a more general concept" being, as we shall describe it by referring to the previously coined term, the "essence of emerging legal obligations". Let us term this view as "legal essentialism". Let us note that

Estreicher used the term of the "essence of law", which, although different, had a very close meaning, e.g.: "These eternal needs and measures are this side of phenomena whose learning leads deeply into the essence of law" (Estreicher 1901, p. 169). Stanisław Estreicher, when rejecting concepts of e.g. the "spirit of nation" or universal psychical features of the homo sapiens, refers here to the common in its forms, although changing in the process of evolution, necessity of assuring mutual help, which generates proper cooperation and, consequently, leads to the exchange of services and goods. The normatively ordered, because of its purely practical purposes, collective social existence is possible on the condition of "keeping good faith to your brother, under the threat of the reaction from all those who are related with you, and under the threat of being excluded from the solidarity and the relationship binding the whole group" (Estreicher 1901, p. 46).

The characteristic reference made by Malinowski to the principle of do ut es as the guarantee of "honest complying with the mutual obligations" is based on the identical—in terms of sense—concept ("principle", "imperative", "rule", etc., depending on the used formulation), the concept fulfilling in keeping the mutuality in all kinds of relationships creating the social order. Thus, in his works, we can easily find formulations in the kind of: "He [the man—ed. K. P.] must cooperate, and cooperation always involves the existence of a group of people, united under one mutual essential regulation, i.e. the set of laws regulating their behavior towards one another"; in primitive cooperation, the main motive is the specified system of mutual obligations (. . .), in which the need for cooperation is accompanied by the understanding of one's own interests, privileges and benefits"; "the principle of mutuality (. . .), systematic interdependence of mutual services makes the basis for the force of law in all human societies (Malinowski 2001, pp. 18, 26, 54). Let us add that for Malinowski "law" in this and many other statements is the term determining all kinds of regulations; in accordance with his unconcealed aversion to attaching too much importance to terms describing different kinds of norms, e.g.: "whether we shall use the term 'law' or whether we shall we replace it with some other expression is of secondary importance. Our own law is nothing else but a custom of essential force, a custom which secures the efficient functioning of our institutions (. . .)" (Malinowski 2001, p. 16).

Forestalling all possible accusations that Bronislaw Malinowski could have "borrowed" (adopted) the above assumptions from the environment different from Krakow legal circles, let us note that "legal essentialism" was typical of virtually all recognized representatives of the German theory and philosophy of law at the end of the nineteenth century, while on Polish lands under the Prussian occupation it was propagated and developed exactly by the "Kraków School of Law", chiefly by Lotar Dargun, and subsequently by Stanisław Estreicher lecturing *ex cathedra* on the *"History of the German State and Law"* (see Patkaniowski 1964, pp. 228 and next, Maneli 1966, pp. 67 and next). Throughout the whole course of World War I, and later in the 1920s, when Bronislaw Malinowski conducted "field research" and created his basic works, he did not maintain (and could not maintain) contacts with any other legal environment with which he would have exchanged thoughts, concepts and views. Hence, it seems that his "legal essentialism" must have originated from the "Kraków" source, from the times when he could listen to deliberations by Stanisław Estreicher. While comparing the well-known criticism leveled by Malinowski against different ethnological concepts of primal forms of marriage (especially the so-called collective marriage), it seems obvious that the arguments he brought forward were almost literally drawn from the concept of the primitive ownership contract, formulated by Stanisław Estreicher.

To conclude, normative (legal) essentialism formulated by both of the scientists reveals the following convictions they shared:

1. Law, as a kind of regulations and normative institutions ("organizations") empirically distinguishable, since the very beginning, accompanied all the organizational forms of human collectivity; it is present in primitive peoples in its "primitive" form, poorly developed, hence difficult to identify, but it still undergoes the process of evolution.
2. The evolution of law is the integral part of the evolution of a given culture.
3. The evolution of culture—and law—is diversified in terms of its pace and other features, but it is possible to "discover" some general models of the evolutionary development of law, common for all societies and epochs.
4. Anywhere, in any collectivity, law emerges together with the possibility of shaping laws and obligations by interested individuals, as a consequence of a certain degree and kind of the level of independence ("empowerment of individuals") achieved by them. The source of contents of legal regulations are different kinds of arrangements between interested individuals, (e.g., contract) or a unilateral reaction of institution of the authority to external threats to the whole community or internal violations of the accepted order.
5. Law emancipates itself (identifies itself and distinguishes) from other normative regulations in the slow, never-ending process. It is the consequence of changes taking place in the way of guaranteeing the obedience to specific rules of conduct by a given community; the rules of conduct become "legal" when in the place of the guarantee of their obeying. based on the necessity of keeping a good opinion (prestige, position) by an individual in his collectivity, the threat of punishment from transcendent beings ("gods"), the fear from being exposed to the punishing reaction of the whole community, there also starts to function an additional and separate guarantee, consisting in introducing sanctions by an institution of the authority (the political authority); the institution being the guardian of obeying those rules of conduct—the rules not necessarily accepted by all members of a given collectivity and not in an equal degree, not "automatically" and not non-exceptionally obeyed by everyone.
6. A phenomenon generating any set of rules of conduct, the "essence of normativity" is observable in each society, regular obedience to the rule of mutuality (reciprocation) by proper acts of exchange in every kind of relationships between members ("elements") of a given community.

2.9 The Open Question

Despite the above deliberations, the importance of Stanisław Estreicher's influence on the research assumptions and concepts formulated by Bronislaw Malinowski is still not a foregone conclusion, especially in reference to those on ethnological research on law. Certainly, however, all that has been observed and merely highlighted in this paper confirms the possibility of such an influence in a degree rejecting the negation of its existence. Further, it allows contemporary anthropologists of law, historians and theoreticians of law—not only in Poland but worldwide—to realize how much their "new" concepts and findings resemble those formulated long ago.

References

Estreicher, S. 1901. *Początki prawa umownego [The beginnings of contract law]*. Kraków: Wydawnictwo Uniwersytetu Jagiellońskiego.

Estreicher, S. 1936. Michał Bobrzyński. *Przegląd Współczesny [The Modern Review]* 1.

Kroeber, A.L. 2009. Istota kultury [The essence of culture]. In: *Świat człowieka-świat kultury [Man's world – A world of culture]*, ed. E. Nowicka, M. Głowacka-Grajper. Warszawa: PWN.

Kurczewski, J. 2012. Petrażycki in Melanezia – Where Pospisil and Malinowski meet. In *Towards an anthropology of the legal field*, ed. T. Ledvinka, K. Varhanik-Wildowa, R.Visinger. Prague: Karolinum Press, Charles University.

Malinowski, B. 1936a. Anthropology. In *Encyclopedia Britannica*, vol. 1. London, New York.

Malinowski, B. 1936b. Introduction. In: *Koczownictwo. Studia nad nomadyzmem i nad wpływem tegoż na społeczeństwo, ustrój i prawo [Study on Nomadism and its impact on society, polity and law]*, ed. F. Gross. Warszawa: Instytut Popierania Nauki.

Malinowski, B. 2001. *Prawo, Zwyczaj, Zbrodnia w Społeczności Dzikich [Crime and custom in savage society]*. Warszawa: De Agostini.

Maneli, M. 1966. *Historia doktryn polityczno-prawnych XIX wieku, Część II [History of the legal and political theory at the XIX century, Part II]*. Warszawa: PWN.

Patkaniowski, M. (ed.). 1964. *Studia z Dziejów Wydziału Prawa Uniwersytetu Jagiellońskiego [Studies on the history of the Faculty of Law and Administration, Jagiellonian Univeristy]*. Kraków: Wydawnictwo Uniwersytetu Jagiellońskiego.

Petrażycki, L. 1925. *O pobudkach postępowania i o istocie moralności i prawa [On the motives of conduct and the essesnce of law and morality]*. Warszawa: Wydawnictwo Uniwersytetu Warszawskiego.

Znamierowski, Cz. 2001. Wstęp [Preface]. In *Prawo, Zwyczaj, Zbrodnia w Społeczności Dzikich [Crime and custom in savage society]*, ed. B. Malinowski. Warszawa: De Agostini.

Part II

Chapter 3
Malinowski's Multidimensional Conception of Law: Beyond Common Misunderstandings

Mateusz Stępień

3.1 Introduction

Bronislaw Malinowski (1884–1942) is undoubtedly one of the titans of social sciences. He strongly influenced the shape of modern cultural anthropology and is considered to be the inventor of the participant observation method. His concepts of language, magic, religion, and culture are still to this day a subject of study and a source of inspiration. However, we cannot say the same about his conception of law. Although Edward A. Hoebel stressed that Malinowski's ideas are a "challenge to the jurisprudence" (1946, p. 851), nobody took up the challenge and, as yet, his conception of law has not even been fairly reconstructed or recapitulated by researchers. There is a huge disparity between the wide reception given to Malinowski's works that are not directly related to law, and the little interest in his legal writings. A glance at the existing literature illustrates how little has been written on Malinowski's Conception of Law (Seagle 1937; Hoebel 1954, pp. 177–210; Schapera 1957; Conley and O'Barr 2002; Kurczewski 2009, 2012; Tuori 2015, pp. 110–117). The few authors that cite his legal thoughts use elements of his conception of law selectively, and Malinowski is virtually ignored by the legal sciences. It is rarely referred to in the legal sciences and only a handful of adherents were truly inspired by his legal thoughts.

Potential exposure to Malinowski's influence has in the main been limited to American legal realism. Laura Kalman believes that it is functionalism—a perspective developed in the mature form by Malinowski himself—that most fully defines the project of the realists (1986, p. 3). In the words of William Seagle, Malinowski's "functionalism, indeed, has exercised a pervasive influence upon modern jurisprudence, and he is really entitled to be regarded as the sire of the

M. Stępień (✉)
Department of Sociology of Law, Jagiellonian University, Krakow, Poland
e-mail: mateusz.stepien@uj.edu.pl

M. Stępień (ed.), *Bronislaw Malinowski's Concept of Law*,
DOI 10.1007/978-3-319-42025-7_3

realists, neo-realists and ultra-realists" (1937, p. 290). In support of Seagle's comment, we can point out a few passages in which legal realists appealed to Malinowski's conception.

Jerome Frank quoted Malinowski in his works, although these were not directly related to law (1930, p. 15). In his considerations of the functional understanding of social institutions, Felix S. Cohen recalled Malinowski's study on Aborigines. Further, when writing about the functional meaning of primitive law, he also relied on *Crime and Customs* (1935, pp. 831, 832). Karl Llewellyn was another reader of Malinowski who received his ideas enthusiastically (1930, p. 436; Llewellyn and Hoebel 1941, p. 27; see Twining 1973, p. 153). Nevertheless, considering the massive impact that works such as *The Argonauts,* had on anthropological studies, Malinowski's legal thoughts had a relatively minor influence on legal realism and there were relatively few direct references to his works. One of the potential reasons for this is that the realist movement began much earlier, drawing its inspiration from other sources (see, for example, Herget and Wallace 1987). Certainly, functionalist thinking also has American roots associated with pragmatism. Moreover, some authors, like Roscoe Pound (1936, p. xxxiv) and Myres S. McDougal (1941, p. 834), were fairly interested in Malinowski's concept of institution, but others such as Nicholas Timasheff (1939, p. 277) were rather critical towards it.

There is a controversy about the influence Malinowski had on development of Talcott Parsons' functional understanding of law and, consequently, the whole tradition derived from him. In Parsons' most famous book, *The Social System*, Malinowski's works are rarely cited, leading some scholars to conclude that Parsons was not significantly influenced by Malinowski (see Gerhardt 2002). However, it can be argued that Parsons' entire theoretical project is based on premises and assumptions developed by Malinowski. In 1924, Parsons attended a course run by Malinowski at the London School of Economics, which he later recalled as having had a big impact on him (1957, p. 54). Clearly, it seems that Malinowski's thoughts influenced Parsons to a much greater extent than it is commonly assumed.

The first part of this chapter is set out to enumerate the factors that affected (and still affect) the little interest shown in Malinowski's Conception of Law. To understand and question some of commonly accepted views and allegations against Malinowski legal conceptions, the chapter also seeks to provide a proper understanding of his project in the context of his contemporaries. Even the most cursory study of the legacy of author of *The Argonauts* indicates his anti-reductionist approach, related to his multidimensional characterization of law. Malinowski developed an original understanding of law as a multidimensional phenomenon, which appears to be incoherent and inconsistent. This leads us to the main purpose of this chapter, which is a reconstruction of Malinowski Conception of Law, based on the Davidsonian Principle of Charity. Please note that criticism and evaluation of Malinowski's conception from the perspectives of both contemporary anthropology of law and legal science are not subjects of this paper.

3.2 Factors Affecting Disinterest in Malinowski's Conception of Law

Anthropologists and sociologists frequently appeal to Malinowski's conceptions. Many textbooks and compendiums of anthropology of law include passages (e.g. Rouland 1994, pp. 36–37, 40) or even chapters (e.g. Donovan 2008, pp. 69–78) dedicated to his legal thought. Malinowski is widely known as a pioneer that "broke the crust of legal formalism in anthropology and gave a new impetus to the anthropology of law" (Hoebel 1954/1967, p. 208). However, there was a little interest in his conceptions within the legal sciences. Harri Engelund described this state as "disciplinary amnesia" (2015, p. 270). This is notable when compared to the works of other classic authors in the social sciences, such as Karol Marx, Emil Durkheim, and Max Weber, which still attract a lot of attention within contemporary legal research. This is even more marked when you consider that Malinowski dedicated his monograph (1926a) and a several papers (1925a, 1925b, 1926b, 1934, 1936b), including his final work published shortly before his death (1942a), precisely to legal matters. In 1940–1941, Malinowski led a seminar on Primitive Jurisprudence at Yale University, shared by the Department of Anthropology and Yale Law School (see Murdock 1942). The significant point here is that his methodological and theoretical approaches had very strong implications for the legal sciences, namely his direct observation of social (particularly legal) practices by participant observation and his functionalist theories. So why were Malinowski's legal thoughts largely ignored? On analysis, there appears to be a number of possible contributory factors.

At the time, discussion within Western jurisprudence focused around a few classic topics. Malinowski never discussed the tension between positive and natural law in his writings, and did not deal with justice at all. He also studied stateless societies and was not concerned with the relationship between law and state. Additionally, Malinowski was not a lawyer, unlike earlier authors such as Johann Jakob Bachofen, Josef Köhler, Henry S. Maine and Lewis H. Morgan, which may have put him at some disadvantage when linking anthropology with jurisprudence, or at least made his work less readily acceptable to legal scholars.

The topics and issues that Malinowski was interested in were already explored by other scholars who were critical of the dominant paradigms of understanding law, namely formal-positivism and natural law. The writings of these scholars (involved in legal realism, sociological jurisprudence, Free Law Movement, etc.) were much more embedded in the discussion within jurisprudence. This circle of criticism narrowed the scope of argumentation and placed such exotic research as Malinowski's beyond limits. Moreover, Malinowski himself never referred to the leading opponents of the dominant paradigms, such as Leon Petrazycki or Eugen Ehrlich, apart from perfunctory mentions of their names (e.g. 1942a, p. 1250). In this sense, he was "marginalized at his own request". Also his position has not been understood in "normal" legal science because of its novelty and ground-breaking character. Sally Moore rightly pointed out that "Malinowski's ideas suffered the common fate of many cultural innovations. When exported from anthropology and introduced into another discipline, jurisprudence, anthropological ideas were interpreted in ways that would disrupt pre-existing jurisprudential schemes as little as possible; they were selectively incorporated, but not used very creatively" (2000, p. 220).

Malinowski's legal thoughts were also associated with the generally perceived weakness of anthropological studies on normative phenomena within so-called primitive societies, especially so when they made hypotheses about law. Indeed, Malinowski himself complained that study in this area "was driven into an impasse of artificial and sterile constructions" (1926a, p. 4; also 1929, p. 26). Unlike previous anthropological studies, Malinowski's a methodological, conceptual and theoretical points of view were scientifically valid. However, the prevailing attitude towards the weakness of claims based on primitive law undoubtedly affected the scale of interest in the anthropology of law by legal science scholars. This was unfortunate, as, compared to his colleagues, Malinowski's work was considerably more advanced. For comparison, let us take a look at two widely quoted authors of that time. In *Ifugao Law,* Roy Barton indicated that "their [Ifugao tribe—ed. M.S.] law is based entirely on custom and taboo" (1919, p. 6). Ifugao have a well-developed legal system, which is, however, "in the first stage of the development of law" (1919, p. 16). Edwin S. Hartland, a friend of Malinowski, defined primitive law as "all the customs of the tribe", "the rules that govern society of lower culture", and "the traditional rule of the community" (1924, pp. 5, 8, 137). In such forms, it is not surprising that Barton and Hartland's remarks were not any challenge for jurisprudence, which was much better conceptually equipped to analyze normative phenomena. In fairness, although Malinowski's account was more mature and richer than those of Barton and Hartland, it still faced similar deficiencies when dealing with normative phenomena.

Another factor that minimized Malinowski's influence on jurisprudence was his manner and style of writing (see Payne 1981). He often entirely disregarded authors he had criticized, presented their theses in trivialized forms, or mentioned opposing theories only after they had long been rejected. Quoting his "enemies" selectively, greatly simplifying their ideas, and wholly ignoring well-known scientific literature frequently led him to an "easy intellectual victory". Clyde Kluckhohn called this attitude "the flogging of dead horses" (1943) and Alfred Radcliffe-Brown referred to it as "the amusement of setting up a straw man for the pleasure of making fun of it and demolishing it" (1935). His tendency to superficial interpretations or even recreating the theses of others for his own ends is particularly evident in his claims on primitive law. Although what could be kindly referred to his "rhetorical method" was it a bit intellectually dishonest, it enabled him write more freely. Most importantly, Malinowski's oversimplifications of the opinions of his opponents led him to his binary thesis. According to Malinowski, the dominant dogma was that "X is Y" (e.g. primitive societies are chaotic), but he was showing that "X is not Y" (e.g. primitive societies are not chaotic, they are well-ordered) (see Sect. 3.3 for more explanation of Malinowski's "dogmas").

The imprecision and conceptual chaos in Malinowski's deliberations were seemingly in conflict with his intellectual profile, as he was raised in neo-positivist paradigm of science (see Flis 1988). However, the neo-positivist approach faced opposition by the artistic side of Malinowski's personality, which was strongly stimulated by his friendship with Polish avant-garde artist Stanislaw Witkiewicz (see e.g. Skalnik 1995). In this way, empiricism and inductionism became integrated with the belief that "artistic sensibility" is part of a good social science (Malinowski 1922, p. 18)—a position Malinowski defended to the end of his scientific career. However, despite his "artistic" inclinations, Malinowski repeatedly wrote about the need to define and separate law from other norms. In his first book in English, written before his fieldwork, he noted that describing primitive law requires "necessary, precise concepts and clear definitions" (1913, p. 10). In *Crimes and Customs,* Malinowski argues that the purpose of his work is to propose a "satisfactory classification of the norms and rules of primitive community" (1926a, p. 15). He dedicated much attention to this issue, including an entire section in *Crimes and Customs* and as a major element of his last paper concerning law (1942a, p. 1238). Unfortunately, Malinowski never fulfilled his promises of developing clear definitions—even *genus proximum* of law was presented in an ambiguous manner. Moreover, when analyzing law, Malinowski did not separate (1) the conditions necessary for its functioning, (2) the effects it causes, and (3) the law itself, which is located between the first two factors.

The manner in which his research was presented did not reflect the need for precision, demarcation and sharp definition, emphasized by Malinowski so many times (Schapera 1957, pp. 139, 146; Conley and O'Barr 2002, p. 864). Even in his mature work, Malinowski did not propose a coherent conceptual framework for legal issues. Moreover, his individual works are characterized by numerous inconsistencies and definitional negligence. Malinowski wrote frivolously about "law", "primitive law", "customary law", "native law", "savage law", "law and order", and "legal forces" in such a way that it is difficult to indicate what kind of relationship he thought might exist between these concepts. In some passages, for instance, Malinowski suggested that "law" is a subcategory of "customs" (1926a, p. 54), while in others he clearly assumed their distinction (1936a, p. 442; 1945, p. 45); occasionally he even used the terms as alternatives (1934, pp. xxviii, xxx, xli). The relationship between "law" and "primitive law" is particularly interesting. The term "primitive" indicates a number of meanings, which were at the time associated with evolutionary thinking (social Darwinism) and which treated concepts such as law to be, in a sense, incomplete or still in development. When Malinowski distinguished primitive law from "crystallized" law (1934, p. xxviii; 1942a, pp. 1236, 1237), he was under the influence of evolutionary thinking that was popular at the time. However, his main project was to identify an infrastructure ("the real mechanism of law") that underlies every law. This he did while studying of the nature of law amongst the people of the Trobriand Islands. From this, he concluded that, so-called Western law is based on the same complex machinery, but with some additional characteristics. Therefore, primitive law is a kind of rudimentary law, while crystallized law is based on the same foundations, but has some additional features. These foundations or core infrastructure are what Malinowski refers to the "minimum definition of law" (1926a, p. 67), or "essential core of each institution [including the law—ed. M.S.]" (1945, p. 54).

Lack of precision and definitional problems also relate to another issue. Malinowski was influenced by a different approach that assumes continuity between the various aspects of the normative sphere within so-called primitive societies. In such a case, these norms can only be distinguished analytically from each other. It explains why Malinowski wrote about the "legal aspect of norms" (1913, p. 16). He pointed out that religious acts and magical institutions have their "legal side" (1926a, pp. 43, 87). In a similar sense, he noted that "the law covers the whole culture and the entire tribal constitution of the natives", and that laws and customs are "organically connected and not isolated" (1926a, pp. 49, 125). Law, if possible to extract at all, is always "unified" with other elements of culture. One of the essential features of his approach is considering culture (which law is part of) as relatively integrated whole (1944/1961, pp. 36, 150). Malinowski did not notice any inconsistencies in this approach, which enables separating law and at the same time not separating law from other norms. As a consequence, and also because of the difficulty in demarcating law, Malinowski's approach was not attractive for the jurisprudence and even less so for legal positivism. Similarly, his proposal did not inspire supporters of more sociologically sound approaches to law because it did not bring any new or strong arguments against the positivist orthodoxy and—focused too much on biology.

3.3 Malinowski's Criticism of Existing Conceptions

Before reconstructing of Malinowski's Conception of Law, we first need to look at the assertions he was working against and which, in his opinion, dominated the literature. We can distinguish five "dogmas", as Malinowski called them, which characterized the dominant stream of discussion on primitive law.

The first dogma concerned the uniqueness of the West, which considers itself to be in possession of the law. Instead of assuming that the normative sphere in primitive societies is "irrational" and "backward", Malinowski showed that there are a number of legal mechanisms that contribute to the maintenance of society as a whole. He questioned the thesis according to which law is a product of very few and therefore privileged societies. This issue is directly related to cultural factors influencing the definition of law in a certain society.

The next dogma concerned group dominance over the individual within so-called primitive societies. It manifests in the thesis of primacy of "group-sentiment" (1926a, pp. 42, 48, 55), "primitive communism" (1926a, pp. 3, 19, 26, 37) and "instinctive submission" (1929, p. 11). In the case of law, there are other theses associated with this dogma, such as "collective responsibility", "group-property" and "group-justice" (1926a, pp. 55, 3). However, Malinowski wrote openly about "the enlightened individual interest," which is characteristic for people living in pre-industrial societies, where mutual obligations are constantly tested and negotiated, as well as violated, in the name of individual benefits. This happens even at the expense of close relatives. Malinowski emphasized the existence of precise rights to ownership among natives (1926a, p. 19). This led him to the conclusion that a native "is neither an extreme nor an intransigent" (i.e. neither a collectivist nor an individualist), but a combination of both (1926a, pp. 56, 127). Later, in *Coral Gardens and their Magic*, he wrote on "undying fallacy of anthropological work – the opposition between communism and individualism" (1935, p. 319).

The third dogma concerned the total impact upon which traditions, customs and norms have on native's behavior. Such traditionalism was a major factor in founding indigenous collectivism. According to this vision, an individual mechanically performs as tradition dictates. Dealing with the myth of "the automatic submission", Malinowski wrote about "the stupid wild" as a fictional construct created by poor anthropologists. According to this myth, "wild" is a radical legalist and conformist, who is obedient to tradition. Malinowski indicated, in turn, that implementing norms in pre-industrial societies does not happen in an automatic and in unreflective way. In the societies he studied, there are free riders and those who violate obligations using bribery and intrigue. This does not mean, however, that "savages" are total anarchists. In many situations, especially when emotions or interests do not push them in another direction, savages act within the commandments of their tradition. Malinowski claimed that conformism and tendency towards satisfying public opinion does not differentiate Malaysians from Europeans. They are also common characteristics for "Eastern European ghettos, Oxford colleges, and Fundamental Middle Eastern Communities" (1926a, p. 52). Conformism is a universal phenomenon and therefore cannot constitute a distinctive feature of "primitive" societies.

Malinowski criticized the dominant perspective that placed emphasis on cases of law and order violations. In his view, "the sociologist and the ethnographer ... primarily must be interested in the working of social control, that is, in the maintenance of order". Jurisprudence should also adopt a "deeper" approach to legal phenomena (1942a, p. 1246). Thus, the most important thing is to study the "relation between the existing law and order in society" (1942a, p. 1247). Because Malinowski was interested in social mechanisms of maintaining order and the role law played in these processes, it is not surprising that he criticized the narrow "definition of law as the machinery of carrying out justice in cases of trespass" (1926a, p. 31). In fact, this is one of his strongest claims. Misconceptions in studies on so-called primitive societies are caused by looking for mechanisms of maintaining order in places where we have got used to seeing them. Malinowski's emphasis on maintaining, rather than restoring, social order was related to his critical approach towards the orthodox position, which recognized a penal nature of primitive law (1926a, pp. 15, 31, 56, 66, 72). Such a view, however, entirely ignores the most important "phenomena of their legal life" (1926a, p. 31). He noted that, in so-called primitive societies, "civil" norms (civil law) are much more developed than penal sectors associated with prohibition. But with typical inconsistency, Malinowski placed the term "Crime" in the title of his monograph.

3.4 Reconstruction of Malinowski's Multi-level Conception of Law

Before trying to reconstruct Malinowski's Conception of Law, it should be noted that his individual works were most often read without any deep analysis of the assumptions upon which his theory of society was based. In order not to make the same mistake, we should place Malinowski's understanding of law against the background of his ontology and epistemology of social life. Some authors have argued that his conception of law "changed several times during the course of his career" (Schapera 1957, p. 139). It is true that there are many inconsistencies and contradictions in Malinowski's writings. But, looking more broadly, we can observe the continuity of his most general claims, epistemological beliefs and theoretical assumptions associated with the understanding of law. Over time, he was constantly loyal to empiricism, induction and the nomothetic vision of (legal) science, although not in its extreme forms. By the end of his scientific career, Malinowski's ontological and epistemological position represented soft naturalism and anti-reductionism, which acknowledged the complex nature of social phenomena, including their biological and psychological dimensions. Malinowski extended his early reflections and intuitions concerning law into a larger theoretical whole. Unfortunately, because of his early death, his theory was not fully developed and remains only in the form of an outline. Hence, there are great difficulties in reconstructing, understanding and interpreting his conception of law. Because of its anti-reductionism, reading Malinowski's works in a one-dimensional way is insufficient. It is a common mistake to put psychological factors associated with reciprocity at the center of his definition of law (e.g. Hoebel 1946, p. 851, 1954, p. 180; Rouland 1994, p. 40; Donovan 2008, pp. 70–71).

Malinowski did not only fight against particular "dogmas", but also developed a conception of law that perfectly fits within his epistemology and ontology of the social world. According to this conception, an adequate analysis of legal phenomena should include the relations between its biological, social and psychological dimensions.

3.4.1 Biological Dimension of Law

Culture is at the center of Malinowski's research. His anthropology is in general a "science of culture". Despite the fact that he wrote explicitly about "cultural determinism", his theses are far from the strong claims characterized by the

Standard Social Science Model (Tooby and Cosmides 1992, pp. 24–49). Malinowski shaped his intellectual profile at the Jagiellonian University in Kraków, which was at the time was greatly influenced by Viennese neo-positivism. There he studied natural science and math, and later, in Leipzig, was considering a post doctoral degree in chemistry before suffering from poor health. During his ethnographic research and the long time spent elaborating his conceptions for publication, Malinowski devoted himself to analyzing the role and character of cultural factors. He then began developing a synthesis based on the assumption that biology is essential for social life—"it is evident that the driving forces of all behavior are biologically conditioned" (1942b, p. 77).

From today's perspective, Malinowski's position is best described as "soft" naturalism. This is because of his emphasis on the biological basis of social life and his belief that biological factors determine culture. According to Malinowski's thinking, culture is a typical way that humans adapt to their environment. Within "the artificial environment of culture", itself a kind of "strengthening physiology", it is possible to satisfy human needs. Thanks to culture, humans act "under the condition of order, continuity and predictability". As a result, people can better deal with specific problems. In this sense, culture is part of human biology.

Malinowski also recognized the existence of a new type of need caused by culture itself. This is directly associated with cultural determinism. Thus, culture is not a passive tool of biological imperatives. Next to the primary needs (animal, basic, biological), there are also the secondary ones (human society and culture) that are "implications of man's cultural responses to innate urges" (1936a, p. 447). In other words, satisfying primary needs creates new, specific, secondary, "cultural" needs, which are rooted in the symbolic world (1942b, p. 77). Therefore, culture is a determined object and, at the same time, it determines human behavior. It should be emphasized that, to Malinowski, needs (see Piddington 1957) link both biology with culture and the psychological with the social dimension. This position still has its followers and can be seen in the tradition associated with the teachings of psychologist Abraham Maslow the hierarchy of needs (e.g. Corning 2000).

Now we can look at how Malinowski defined the place of law. He noted that most laws are the expression "of some sound biological reality" and "of some important and functionally founded trend of culture" (1934, pp. lxvi; xxxii). This passage already indicates the duality of law. Firstly, it is a tool for survival and satisfying biological imperatives. Law "is not an end in itself, but an indispensable instrument for the achievement of the real, biological ends within human activities" (1942a, p. 1245). Secondly, as pointed out by Malinowski in his earlier works: "the fundamental function of law is to curb certain natural propensities", "control human instincts" and to enforce non-spontaneous coercive behaviors (i.e. to make people conform) (1926a, p. 64). Following this path, he also recognized law as a way of "limiting" biological imperatives (1942a, p. 1245). In this sense, we are dealing with a clear tension between treating law both as a tool of expressing natural inclinations and as a way of limiting them. While Malinowski did not develop this idea directly, we can say that, as a cultural creation, law can facilitate the implementation of certain biological imperatives, as well as limit or reduce their impact of the same or other biological imperatives. The question is, which inclinations of human nature need protection, and which should be restricted by law, and what kind of relation exists between the two. Furthermore, we should also consider whether the implementation of a significant number of biological needs (which are not fully harmonized or compatible with each other) does not require restrictions in implementing others (i.e. to create balance and order)?

To Malinowski, law, even as an element of culture, cannot be described or explained without its biological ground. Nowadays, there is a huge enterprise of socio-biological studies and the link between social and natural sciences has been established. Malinowski's "soft" naturalism is therefore notable and its general character still gives it potential relevance today. It is of importance that he did not make two fundamental errors. The first is the error of biological reductionism (limiting culture to a mere instrumental role, explaining cultural facts by referring only to biological factors). The second error is that of cultural reductionism, declaring total self-determination and cultural independence in accordance with *omnis cultura ex cultura*. Some authors accused Malinowski of undue biological inclinations (e.g. Radcliffe-Brown 1949, p. 320), while others appreciated his "greatest theoretical effort" (Parsons 1957, p. 56). It seems, however, that his claims, avoiding both "reductionisms" and connecting (although not identifying) the world of nature with human society, followed the right direction.

3.4.2 Social Dimension of Law

Apart from biological factors, Malinowski also considered social factors. He dedicated most of his scientific attention to them. In the case of primitive law, his early thoughts were particularly inspired by sociology. From the beginning, he drew attention to the kind of sanctions that distinguish law from other norms. This does not mean that he defended the position that defined law by organized coercion and force. Malinowski was looking for the specific ways in which law applies sanctions, which, for him, meant a syndrome of factors causing the norms to be actually binding. Consequently, he did not try to define law by organized violence or force assigned to a central authority. Malinowski characterized law as an "organized, more or less regulated and active social sanction". In his mature works, he presents the view that a norm has legal character if it "is enforced by a direct, organized, and definite social action" (1913, pp. 11, 15). In the case of law, Malinowski wrote about the necessity of the "purposeful, organized and effectively working system of human activities" (1942a, p. 1245); "by law, in the sense of a socially established rule, I mean a command or rule of conduct sanctioned by organized constraints" (1944/1961, p. 175). One of the essential elements of law is its internal, stable and organized infrastructure that makes its norms binding. At the same time, the machinery of law cannot be based on sanctions rooted in supernatural belief or sanctions related to "friendship", "loyalty" or "devotion" (1926a, p. 53). Unfortunately, Malinowski did not offer any positive characterization of sanctions related to legal norms. As a result, when distinguishing religious or moral norms from legal ones, he is using unclear criteria. Furthermore, it is easy to find examples of customary norms that are also based on the "social enforcement system" and are not related to sanctions characteristic of religious and moral norms. In other words, as long as we can still defend the general position of distinguishing legal norms from religious and moral norms through various ways of applying sanctions, the difficulty in separating law from customs is still a serious problem for Malinowski's conception.

A distinctive feature of Malinowski's approach is changing the perspective from which law is seen—from history, origin or form of law—to the effects it has on the functioning of certain elements of culture and its maintenance of culture as a whole. Malinowski was not interested in legal instruments as such, but only in the way "they function in actual life" (1926a, p. 125). For functional thinking, the real consequences caused by a particular institution are more important than its normative shape. Although Malinowski studied the functions performed by (primitive) law, broad reflections on this point are difficult to find in his work. Nevertheless, *Crime and Custom* includes a thesis according to which the general function of law is to make people keep their commitments and, in consequence, enable primary and secondary needs to be satisfied. The main goal of law is to provide continuity of mutual services and to enable people to fulfill their obligations. Malinowski emphasized the necessity of the existence of "tribal law and custom, which has to be established and maintained to keep the whole chain of activities running smoothly", or the protection "of the smooth running of organized behavior" (1944/1961, pp. 98, 104). Although he did not formulate it straightforwardly, it seems that the general function of law is to enable cooperation, which, in turn, becomes an important tool for satisfying human needs. Treating social control as a function of law (1944/1961, pp. 6, 125), should probably be interpreted in a similar manner as providing conditions for cooperation.

Malinowski's analyses were rooted in the idea of achieving and maintaining a macro social state that will satisfy human needs through a variety of cultural mechanisms. Law is the functional context, which emphasizes its importance in developing an infrastructure for cooperation and, at the same time, marginalizing violation cases. Malinowski's purpose was to describe and explain law as a part of system of elements of culture interconnected in a diverse and dynamic way. He considered the real consequences of law's functions law in the context of the possibilities (or lack of them) of satisfying human needs. He also analyzed law according to its impact on the maintenance and functioning of other institutions, but he paid less attention to its nature, origins and formal features. This resulted in the aforementioned problems in defining law.

Certainly, Malinowski did not commit the functionalist fallacy in that all social institutions exist because they serve certain functions to the society in which they are practiced. When analyzing law as part of the Trobriand's social world, he took a heuristic hypothesis of its functionality, knowing that there might be other possibilities (1926a, p. 74; 1936a, p. 449; 1944/1961, p. 170). He pointed out that the world of culture is not consistent, but rather a dynamic whole within which there are also some contradictions. Culture is not a perfectly harmonized whole in which the individual elements are uniquely functional. According to Malinowski's approach, it must be determined empirically in each situation as to whether some functions are fulfilled or not. However, he paid less attention to directly observing social practices that are dysfunctional or neither functional nor dysfunctional.

3.4.3 Psychological Dimension of Law

Emphasizing the fundamental importance of biology and social factors, Malinowski knew exactly how important psychological elements were. During his fieldwork, he left behind the sociological perspective developed by his British mentors. In *A Diary in the Strict Sense of the Term* we can observe a slow path leading Malinowski to acknowledging that the reconstruction of the "main passions, motives and objectives of the" natives is fundamental for his studies, and, as he wrote, is "the essence of research" (2008, p. 477). Social phenomena cannot be described and explained adequately without a complementary analyses relating to the "correlate of consciousness". Norms are also always related to "the natives' views and opinions and utterances (. . .) ideas, feelings, and impulses" (1922, p. 17). Without their understanding, normative phenomena in its various forms cannot be described nor explained. Malinowski was often criticized for his psychological tendency (Parsons 1957, p. 53). Such an allegation is wrong because one of his essential principles was anti-reductionism. Malinowski developed such an approach in *Crime and Customs*. He noted that to classify norms we need to refer to the "motives and sanctions by which they are enforced" (1926a, p. 50). With the exception of sanctions, Malinowski stressed the role of the psychological element, another important and original factor in his thought. In this way, he emphasized that other types of norms are based on different mental processes than law. The feature that distinguishes legal norms is that they "stand out from the rest in that they are felt and regarded as the obligations of one person and the rightful claims of another" (1926a, p. 55). These unique experiences have to be one of the factors that make law different. The question about the possible influence of Leo Pertrazycki, who described law in very similar terms of bilateral imperative-attributive emotional experiences, is beyond the scope of this paper (see Motyka 1999; Kurczewski 2009, 2012).

The elements indicated by Malinowski should not be treated as mutually exclusive—law is a social mechanism "which is to be found at the bottom of all the real obligations" (1926a, p. 62), not just a specific mental experience. Summarizing his own intellectual approach, Malinowski emphasized that he gave up "one-sided" sociological and psychological analyses. Considering "organized systems of human behavior", he stressed that he did not reject the "considerations of individual psychology" (1942b, p. 73; 1944/1961, pp. 6, 23). Thus, "feeling and recognizing" specific claims without the accompanying factors associated with social organization is not sufficient for an adequate definition of law. Similarly, a real "social enforcement system" cannot exist without complementary acts of consciousness. In short, motivation and consciousness were just as important elements of law as "social organization" (1942b, p. 73). Eliminating one of these elements would make the full description and explanation of law impossible. Malinowski was interested in what was happening in the minds of social actors, but he was also fascinated by order in human activities (conscious and unconscious) and its consequences for the social world and the society as a whole. However, there is no accurate definition of relations between social organization, which guarantee that norms are binding, and specific mental experiences.

3.5 Recapitulation

In 1913 Malinowski defined law only by the way it applies sanctions. In *Crime and Custom*, not rejecting his previous conclusions, he emphasized the role of mental experiences. In his later works, law is treated as one of many possible tools of satisfying human needs, most of which are the result of biological factors. For Malinowski, the "social enforcement system" and mental experiences based on reciprocity constitute a syndrome used to fulfill certain functions, leading mainly to satisfying biological needs. Malinowski did not offer an explicit definition of law including the biological (satisfying needs), social (stable social machinery which fulfills certain functions) and psychological aspect (mental states associated with mutual obligations). However, the reconstruction of his thoughts shows that such an approach is compatible with his general assumptions about the ontology and epistemology of social world. Malinowski's basic idea is quite evident: law is a multidimensional bio-sociological-psychological phenomenon that should be examined on all three levels. Certainly, searching for a multifaceted explanation caused many difficulties in his analyses of (primitive) law as a tool for satisfying human needs. Malinowski was perfectly right in criticizing the one-dimensional approach to understanding law, but he failed to develop a satisfactory theory linking the three dimensions. As a consequence, he "paid" a significant price for it, including over-complicating and clouding his original thoughts

These analyses and reconstructions allow us to reduce Malinowski's conception of law to several related claims.

1. Law is a universal element of culture present in every society.
2. We can distinguish a universal legal infrastructure and its particular diverse forms.
3. This core infrastructure is best seen in so-called primitive societies, where the system of law is less complex.
4. Thus, without prejudging whether there is any direction of social evolution, we need to distinguish primitive law from various forms of crystallized law.
5. The rudimentary legal infrastructure, like any other element of culture, consists of interrelated biological, social and psychological phenomena.

6. Law is, therefore, a complex phenomenon which manifests in mind as specific acts of consciousness. It includes the social enforcement system used at least to fulfill the function of enabling people to co-operate.
7. By fulfilling this function, law indirectly satisfies human biological needs.
8. Law must, however, often restrain people from satisfying certain biological needs to satisfy others (or the same needs by other people).
9. There are also conflicts between biological and secondary needs satisfied through law, resulting from culture-based needs that sometimes become autonomous.
10. In principle, and it is a heuristic hypothesis, law is an instrument of satisfying biological needs of members of some society, but it can be used for other purposes (e.g. satisfying cultural needs or satisfying individual needs at the expense of the collective needs).

3.6 Summary

Malinowski's approach was inclusive and broad, combining perspectives which many other scholars found incoherent. He did not distinguish between consciousness and actions on an individual level and those of a group or society. When explaining the phenomena of social reality, he used both perspectives. Malinowski's works have been an inspiration for theories that were not originally interested in intentions and motivations, but in maintenance of social systems. Notable examples include Parson's System Theory and Luhmann's Autopoietic Theory. At the same time, his works have been an inspiration for approaches oriented towards interpretive analysis of social life. "From the Inside" and "From the Native's Point of View" had a marked influence on interpretative anthropology, ethnomethodology, and folk psychology. In the social sciences, he established grounds for developing the "etic" (investigating what people think) and "emic" (observing and interpreting what people do) methodologies for fieldwork. Moreover, Malinowski presented strong arguments against building a "great ditch" between the world of nature and social world (between natural science and social science). In his writings he emphasized the instrumental character of cultural elements in respect to biological imperatives. However, nowhere is his mission was any desire or attempt to reduce the social world to biology.

Malinowski's multidimensional conception of law, based on above mentioned assumptions, provides a very interesting new insight into how law functions. Undoubtedly, it has much greater descriptive and explanatory potential than other anthropological conceptions developed before the 1940s, perhaps later. From a methodological and theoretical point of view, his legal venture was an innovative project. For sure, it may leave us a little unsatisfied. His claims are in many places chaotic and inconsistent. Interesting hypotheses are only signaled, and intellectually stimulated reader might feel disappointed. However, Malinowski's legal thoughts provide plenty of fodder from which to formulate interesting research questions and are still a good foundation from which to create better theories that might describe and explain how law functions, based on new findings within the social and natural sciences.

References

Barton, R.F. 1919. *Ifugao law*. Berkeley: University of California Press.
Cohen, F. 1935. Transcendental nonsense and the functional approach. *Columbia Law Review* 35: 809–849.
Conley, J.M., and M.W. O'Barr. 2002. Back to the Trobriands: The enduring influence of Malinowski's crime and custom in savage. *Society Law & Social Inquiry* 27(4): 847–874.
Corning, P.A. 2000. Biological adaptation in human societies: A 'Basic Needs' approach. *Journal of Bioeconomics* 2: 41–86.
Donovan, J.M. 2008. *Legal anthropology. An introduction*. Lanham: Altamira Press.
Engelund, H. 2015. Law, law everywhere. *Hau: Journal of Ethnographic Theory* 5(3): 267–271.
Flis, A. 1988. Cracow philosophy at the beginning of the twentieth century and the rise of Malinowski's scientific ideas. In *Malinowski between two worlds: The Polish roots of anthropological tradition*, ed. R. Ellen et al., 105–127. Cambridge: Cambridge University Press.
Frank, J. 1930. *Law and the modern mind*. New York: Brentano's.
Gerhardt, U. 2002. *Talcott Parsons: An intelectual biography*. Cambridge and New York: Cambridge University Press.
Hartland, E.S. 1924. *Primitive law*. London: Methuen.
Herget, J.E., and S. Wallace. 1987. The German free law movement as the source of American legal realism. *Virginia Law Review* 73(2): 399–455.
Hoebel, E.A. 1946. Law and Anthropology. *Virginia Law Review* 32(4): 835–54.
Hoebel, E.A. 1954. The Trobriand Islanders: Primitive law as seen By Bronislaw Malinowski. In *The law of primitive man, a study in comparative legal dynamics*, 177–210. Cambridge: Harvard University Press.
Kalman, L. 1986. *Legal realism at Yale 1927-1960*. Chapel Hill: University of North Carolina Press.
Kluckhohn, C. 1943. Bronislaw Malinowski, 1884–1942. *The Journal of American Folklore* 56 (221): 208–219.
Kurczewski, J. 2009. Bronisław Malinowski misunderstood or how Leon Petrazycki's concept of law is unwittingly applied in anthropology of law. *Societas/Communitas* 1(7): 47–62.
Kurczewski, J. 2012. Petrażycki in Malanesia – where Pospisil and Malinowski meet. In *Towards an athropology of the legal field*, ed. Tomas Ledvinka, Katerina Varhanik-Wildova, et al., 64–77. Prague: Fakulta Humanitních Studií Univerzity Karlovy v Praze.
Llewellyn, K., and A. Hoebel. 1941. *The Cheyenne way: Conflict and case law in primitive jurisprudence*. Norman, OK: University of Oklahoma Press.
Llwellyn, K.N. 1930. A realistic jurisprudence - The next step. *Columbia Law Review* 30(4): 431–465.
Malinowski, B. 1913. *The family among the Australian aborigines: A sociological study*. London: University of London Press.
Malinowski, B. 1922. *Argonauts of the Western Pacific: An account of native enterprise and adventure in the Archipelagos of Melanesian New Guinea*. London: Routledge and Kegan Paul.
Malinowski, B. 1925a. The forces of law and order in a primitive community. *Proceedings of the Royal Institution of Great Britain* 24: 529–547.
Malinowski, B. 1925b. Review of: Primitive law, by E. Sidney Hartland. *Nature* 116: 230–235.
Malinowski, B. 1926a. *Crime and custom in savage society*. New York: Harcourt, Brace & Co.

Malinowski, B. 1926b. Primitive law and order. *Nature* 117: 9–16.
Malinowski, B. 1929. Practical anthropology. *Journal of the International African Institute* 2(1): 22–38.
Malinowski, B. 1934. Introduction. In *Law and order in Polynesia*, H.I. Hogbin. London: Christophers A. C.
Malinowski, B. 1935. *Coral gardens and their magic: A study of the methods of tilling the soil and of agricultural rites in the Trobriand Islands*. London: Allen & Unwin.
Malinowski, B. 1936a. Culture as a determinant of behavior. *The Scientific Monthly* 43(5): 440–449.
Malinowski, B. 1936b. Primitive law. *Man* 36.
Malinowski, B. 1942a. A new instrument for the study of law – Especially primitive. *The Yale Law Journal* 51(8): 1237–1254.
Malinowski, B. 1942b. Man's culture and man's behavior. *Sigma Xi Quarterly* 29(3/4): 182–196.
Malinowski, B. 1944/1961. *A scientific theory of culture and others essays*. London, Oxford, New York: Oxford University Press.
Malinowski, B. 1945. *The dynamics of culture change: An inquiry into race relations in Africa*. New Haven: Yale University Press.
McDougal, M.S. 1941. Fuller vs. the American legal realists: An intervention. *Yale Law Journal* 50: 827–840.
Moore, Sally. 2000. *Law as process: An anthropological approach*. Münster: LIT Verlag Münster.
Motyka, K. 1999. Beyond Malinowski: Petrazycki's contribution to legal pluralism. In *Papers of the XIth international congress of folk law and legal pluralism: Societies in transformation*, ed. K. Benda-Beckmann and H.W. Finkler, 330–337. Moscow: Institute of Ethnology and Anthropology.
Murdock, G.P. 1942. Bronislaw Malinowski. *Yale Law Journal* 51: 1235–1236.
Parsons, T. 1957. Malinowski and the theory of social systems. In *Man and culture: An evaluation of the work of Bronislaw Malinowski*, ed. R. Firth, 53–70. New York: The Humanities Press.
Payne, H.C. 1981. Malinowski's style. *Proceedings of the American Philosophical Society* 125(6): 416–440.
Piddington, R. 1957. Malinowski's theory of needs. In *Man and culture: An evaluation of the work of Bronislaw Malinowski*, ed. R. Firth, 33–52. New York: The Humanities Press.
Pound, R. 1936. Introduction. In *Fundamental principles of the sociology of law*, ed. E. Ehrlich. Cambridge: Harvard University Press.
Radcliffe-Brown, A.R. 1935. Primitive law. *Man* 35: 47–48.
Radcliffe-Brown, A.R. 1949. Functionalism: A protest. *American Anthropologist* 51(2): 320–322.
Rouland, N. 1994. *Legal anthropology*. London: The Athlone Press.
Schapera, I. 1957. Malinowski's theories of law. In *Man and culture: An evaluation of the work of Bronislaw Malinowski*, ed. R. Firth, 139–155. New York: The Humanities Press.
Seagle, W. 1937. Primitive law and Professor Malinowski. *American Anthropologist* 39(2): 275–290.
Skalnik, P. 1995. Bronislaw Kasper Malinowski and Stanislaw Ignacy Witkiewicz: Science versus art in the conceptualization of culture. In *Fieldwork and footnotes. Studies in the history of European anthropology*, ed. H.F. Vermeulen and A. Alvarez Roldán, 129–142. New York and London: Routledge.
Timasheff, N. 1939. *Sociology of law*. New Brunswick, NJ: Transaction Publishers.
Tooby, J., and L. Cosmides. 1992. *The adapted mind: Evolutionary psychology and the generation of culture*. Oxford: Oxford University Press.
Tuori, K. 2015. *Lawyers and savages. Ancient history and legal realism in the making of legal anthropology*. London: Routledge.
Twining, W. 1973. *Karl Llewellyn and the realist movement*. Cambridge: Cambridge University Press.

Chapter 4
Bronislaw Malinowski and the Anthropology of Law

Tomáš Ledvinka

4.1 Introduction

This chapter points out that a solid understanding of Bronislaw Malinowski's relationship to law should be founded on how it differs from both non-legal anthropology and jurisprudence. The reader is guided to the moment when the link between law, anthropology and exotic fieldwork became a fount of inspiration. With a slight retrospective bias, the main lines of research are described as being in favour of Malinowski. A closer look at native law through participant observation acts as a starting point for explaining how the ethnographer sees law within the seamless web of the foreign culture. The symmetrical treatment of law and science should help to illuminate the significance of Malinowski's anthropology of law for those anthropologists who are usually not concerned with law. Reciprocity is presented as a part of a much different idea than the definition of law or *kula*, and as a disconnecting factor in relation to conventional modern dualisms. The chapter then discusses the unrecognised discoveries that are to be found underneath the hostile criticism of Malinowski and the misunderstood ironies expressed by Malinowski within the context of conflict between the Trobriand legal systems as a key to understanding Malinowski's approach to native and European law. Finally, the chapter returns to the impact of Malinowski's methodological innovations, such as cross-cultural comparison and participant observation, on the anthropological ideas of law and legal comparisons.

T. Ledvinka (✉)
Charles University, Faculty of Humanities, Prague, Czech Republic
e-mail: tomas.ledvinka@fhs.cuni.cz

M. Stępień (ed.), *Bronislaw Malinowski's Concept of Law*,
DOI 10.1007/978-3-319-42025-7_4

4.2 Malinowski as a Disciplinary Other

"Following Malinowski, we are soon 'paddling on the lagoon, watching the natives under the blazing sun at their garden work, following them through the patches of jungle; and (. . .) on the winding beaches and reefs, we shall learn about their [law—ed. T.L.]'" (Redfield 1948, p. vii). "The reader may be surprised to learn that he has met law on his placid trip on the lagoon; he may think he has not perceived it. However, he is assured that law in Malinowski's terms is there" (Hoebel 1954, p. 180). This remarkable but ingenuous connection between law and the tropical lagoon has changed how anthropology understands not only tropical "Others", but also law in general. Although unusual enough to inspire a new anthropological approach for which a native canoe is just as relevant a legal and organisational principle as the constitution of modern states, this new situating of law was still too unintelligible for conventional jurisprudence, which is firmly entrenched within conventional disciplinary boundaries. It thus seems that although Malinowski's engagement with social and cultural anthropology reflects the success of a man who managed to synthesise two traditions—strictly empirical science with its first-hand observations and the various subjects of study of armchair anthropology—his engagement with law as an anthropological subject was somewhat out of focus and misrepresented by many. Such an impression is almost inevitable when going through the dozens of subsequent references to Malinowski and law. They could contain a legitimate criticism—one that perhaps comes from differing disciplinary perspectives, but unfortunately they can hardly help us to truly understand his main discoveries about law which have been overlooked until the present. For a complete overview of Malinowski's contributions to the anthropological studies of law see Hoebel (1954, pp. 177–178) or Schapera (1957/1960).

As we are moving through a complicated terrain along a disciplinary border, we should distinguish at least three areas in which the topic of Malinowski and law should be relevant: jurisprudence (or legal science in the broader sense), non-legal anthropology, and in particular the anthropology of law. Jurisprudence's response to Malinowski was more than conservative. Although it has been suggested many times, for instance by Moore, that "this [Malinowski's] breadth of approach applied to a narrow field of observation seems particularly appropriate to the study of law and social change in complex societies," (Moore 2000, p. 55) legal scholars have often labelled Malinowski's studies as merely "exotic" or "historic" instead of "modern-day" or "proximate". Perhaps this was a by-product of the juristic treatment of law as if it were beyond analysis of culture and society. Although there has been certain optimism concerning "the rapprochement between anthropology and jurisprudence" (Bohannan 1967, pp. 47–48), in hindsight Moore was quite sceptical: "Malinowski's ideas suffered the common fate of many cultural innovations. When exported from anthropology and introduced into another discipline, jurisprudence, anthropological ideas were interpreted in ways that would disrupt pre-existing jurisprudential schemes as little as possible; they were selectively incorporated, but not used very creatively" (Moore 2000, p. 220). Also, an anthropology that does not consider the ethnographic theorising of law has much in common with jurisprudence because it can use only the other channel at its disposal, the one by which legal (or rather, conventional juristic) understanding is uncritically transferred into anthropology's understanding of law. The avoidance of both Malinowski and later anthropology of law of the twentieth century thus returns anthropologists to the earlier disciplinary order between law (which was seen normatively) and culture (whose definition was changing at the time)—in other words, to a time before Malinowski, who was a cultural and disciplinary innovator and obviously also the destroyer of the old scientific worldview. For many people, however, the nineteenth-century boundary between law and anthropology still functions as a constraint which keeps empirical science outside the gates of normativity.

For these reasons, I believe that our capacity for understanding Malinowski and the law increases if we see Malinowski as a disciplinary *Other* rather than as a disciplinary *same*. It has not been always recognised that Malinowski was simply not a jurist; he was very different from legal theoreticians. As a result, his work has not been successfully translated into legal theory. The question is whether such a translation is desirable or possible, for the gap remains: The gap between a single anthropologist whose unusual experience with law comes from his anthropological (rather than juristic) background and from his encounter with the law of a remote Melanesian society on the one hand, and thousands or rather millions of jurists educated in more or less the same way at modern law schools all around the world on the other hand. This gap can be also seen in terms of the disparity between the quality of first-hand research and the quantity of transmitted knowledge, or between anthropology's emphasis on experience and the juristic emphasis on apodictic contemplations (with many legal fictions as propositions). Malinowski should not be presented as a neutralised quasi-jurist. However, Malinowski's "legal" achievements are today subject to "disciplinary amnesia" (Engelund 2015, p. 270) not only in the legal sciences but also in the non-legal anthropology.

The anthropology of law, which connects both of those disciplinary traditions, has grown and matured since Malinowski's time, and so this discipline represents perhaps the only safe ground for an objective look back at his significance. In this field, Malinowski was considered one of the first to attempt to fill the "'legal' vacuum in the ethnological literature" (Pospíšil 1973, p. 537)—which had previously been the rule in anthropology—and he certainly was the first to analytically think about the law and legal comparisons with the assistance of participant observation. For this reason he is—alongside a small number of others including Karl Llewellyn and Leopold Pospíšil—an emblematic figure for the subsequent development of the anthropology of law. Within this disciplinary canon, we encounter basically three types of references to Malinowski—recognition of his significance (but without deeper reasoning), theoretical criticism (although usually unfair and misdirected), and empirical remarks that compare his conclusions about law to the conclusions made by the paper in question. The first approach can be illustrated through a few examples. According to Robert Redfield, "the road to the left has been recently opened with a great flourish by B. Malinowski (1926, 1934)"

(1967, p. 3). June Starr claimed that "Malinowski (...) pointed the way towards the empirical study of law by suggesting the ethnographer should not take too narrow a view, so that law is only equated with 'law-breaking'" (1992, p. xxiv). Sally Moore mentioned that "it was not until Malinowski's *Crime and Custom in Savage Society* (1926) that anything written on law by an anthropologist achieved a wide audience and raised serious theoretical questions" (2000, p. 218), and perhaps more generally Laura Nader recognised Malinowski as the one who "broke ground with what today would be called multi-sited fieldwork, and scientific rigor" (2011, p. 214). One example of the second type of reference to Malinowski is criticism of the "overinclusiveness" of Malinowski's definition of law, as first uttered by Redfield (1967, p. 4) and perhaps most recently repeated by Donovan and Anderson (2003), pp. 11–12). Malinowski's theory was seen also as "an outstanding example of the neglecting of the formal aspects of law", for he rejected "the importance of formal characteristics, especially of organised sanction" (de Jong 1948, pp. 4, 7). His concepts of law were accused of containing "various instances of inconsistency and contradiction" (Schapera 1957/1960, p. 146). The last sort of reference to Malinowski is the rarest. Llewellyn and Hoebel (1941), pp. 251, 266–267), for instance, compared the role of reciprocity in Cheyenne and Trobriand law. Further, Hoebel (1967, p. 187) later compared reciprocity among the Comanche to Trobriand reciprocity.

Jan Josselin de Jong, a leading figure of Dutch anthropology at the time, offered still another view on Malinowski: "It seems very strange indeed that Malinowski while sharply criticising [the notion of savage law – ed. T.L.] did not realise that his own description of [Trobriand society—ed. T.L.] did not by any means refute the rejected view, but on the contrary confirmed it (. . .). His own vision had become blurred and so, with regard to the central problem, we are left exactly where we are" (1948, pp. 5–7). Malinowski indeed blurred the categories of law he used. But we should read this blurring as a theoretical implication for legal thought grounded in his fieldwork. The law of the Trobriand lagoons offered not only the gradual addition of new facts to existing knowledge, but also the gradual abandonment of entrenched legal categories. Malinowski's theoretical ideas of law can be thus seen as disconnecting factors (to borrow and modify the concept of private international law) on the road of anthropology's emancipation from normative science.

4.3 Lines of Research

Malinowski followed "the generation of anthropologists working at the turn of the century, such as Alfred C. Haddon, William Rivers, Charles G. Seligman and Baldwin Spencer, who made the first intensive field studies", and together with Alfred R. Radcliffe-Brown established "intense personal fieldwork" and "synchronic analysis" "as academic disciplines" (Nakai 1994, p. 22). Although he had early followers such as Zach Richards and his study of the subsistence lifestyle of the South-eastern Bantu, Ian Hogbin and Wogeo land tenure, Monica Wilson and the Nyakyusa legal system, and Isaac Schapera and Southern Bantu law (Hoebel 1951, p. 248), the theoretical implications of his innovative approach were only realised gradually during the turbulent years of legal anthropology after World War II. The synchronicity of this process and events in world history such as the Nuremberg trials and decolonisation that weakened conventional legal doctrines and entrenched legal categories lent his ideas relevance far beyond disciplinary boundaries.

Although Malinowski was not the only anthropologist to study native law at the time, his liberation from the conventional legal dualisms of Western vs. Savage, civil vs. criminal, substantive vs. processual, public vs. private, or secular vs. religious was unique and remains unrecognised to this day. This chapter looks at Malinowski's early liberation from established ways of thinking about law and tries to show that it was an implicit crucible for later legal anthropologists. However, in retrospect it may be difficult to distinguish which ideas in Malinowski's work were undeveloped seeds that provided inspiration for later enquiries, and which can be justly ascribed to Malinowski himself. Some lines of research can be associated with his name to varying degrees. First, there is the line of research that describes law as a native knowledge that can be identified through the classical anthropology of law (Llewellyn and Hoebel 1941; Pospíšil 1958; Bohannan 1957; Gluckmann 1955; Nader 1990; Offner 1983; French 1995; Rosen 1989). Then there are ethnographic studies of unofficial law in so-called state societies (Abel 1982; Conley and O'Barr 1990; Greenhouse et al. 1994). A third example are studies of the sociocultural context of modern official law, which can be found in the whole body of the sociology of law that is concerned with the sociological aspects of law (for instance Macaulay 1963, 1995; Conley and O'Barr 1997). Fourth are recent ethnographies of Western official law itself (Latour 2002; Riles 2011), and fifth comes that line of research linking the study of non-modern legal systems and other forms of social control with similar studies of the West. Further, finally there is the inter-cultural comparative treatment of legal systems, which is broader than comparative law in the strict sense and which, with a few exceptions, is mostly found alongside the previous examples (Pospíšil 1971; Gluckmann 2012).

At least, all these lines of research follow Malinowski's initial impetus and engage in a far-reaching transformation of the anthropological understanding of law. This transformation could also be seen in this way: when studying savage law, modern law, religious law, or customary law, we should simply erase the modifier so that we are left with just the concept of law. This aspect of Malinowski's approach was deployed by Edwin Hutchins (1980). His half-legal and half-cognitive ethnography was an empirical re-examination of the legal dimension of *Coral Gardens and Their Magic* (1935), with a focus on land tenure. Hutchins saw cultural and legal systems as an embodiment of certain logic of inference situated within specific mental and material settings. In his study, Hutchins realised that a major problem in understanding the real differences between legal systems and thoughts is that "much of discourse is composed of syllogisms in which one or more premises are left unstated" and that ethnographically informed research can provide us with "the premises missing from the discourse itself". The task thus is to specify "the premises on which the inferences are based" (Hutchins 1979, p. 14). If we read Hutchins carefully, we realise that the missing premises also include legal rules on which actors make their decisions. Therefore, if we do not know the laws of a certain culture or its beliefs about the world, then the characterisation of legal thinking as being fundamentally "rational or irrational, concrete or abstract, affective and integrative or rational and analytical, textual or oral" (Hutchins 1979: 13) is probably highly deceptive. Hutchins expressed this notion in his own way: "while Trobrianders' beliefs about the world are, in some domains, very different from our own beliefs, it is unwarranted to infer from a difference in content that the way Trobrianders reason about what they believe is substantially different from the way we reason about what we believe" (Hutchins 1979, p. 16). Hutchins's rethinking of *Coral Gardens*' legal dimension as "a missing cultural premise" within Malinowski's transcriptions of religious narratives and magic formulas demonstrates the significance of Malinowski's own attempts at abandoning certain aspects of modern legal thought that cannot be applied in foreign cultural environment. Besides, the concept of "belief about the world", applied in relation to Malinowski's ethnographies, can be compared with Yan Thomas's concept of *fictio legis* (1995) which shares in this respect the "essence" of certainty-making in empirically uncertain situations.

4.4 Too Broad, Too Narrow or Rather Law Within the Seamless Web of the Foreign Culture?

However, it would be imprecise to say that Malinowski simply denied the conventional legal dualisms of the time. A more correct assessment would be to say that his own methodology, employed in the study of his ethnographic field, acted as a disconnecting factor. If taken to its logical conclusion, the anthropological deployment of the imperative of exact empirical proof (as embodied by the method of participant observation) clearly demonstrates that conventional legal dualisms are useless in ethnographic fieldwork (despite legal theory's claims of general applicability), because it sticks to "our" legal practices and "our" legal institutions. The appearance of general applicability thus remains valid only if a modern legal theory maintains its distance from the legal systems of the Other. The conventional legal dualisms that many social scientists considered universally applicable in nineteenth- and early twentieth-century anthropology were also simply too connected to the central governments, courts, codes and constables—leading them to implicitly claim that every culture must possess the same sorts of courts, codes and constables as modern culture. The way in which the legal dualisms were constructed made these modern legal attributes universal and thus, eo ipso, legitimate—and by correlation, any law that did not possess the same or at least very similar attributes was not recognised or only semi-recognised as Law. The ethnographer's focus was thus subject to this kind of hierarchisation. As a result, the methodology that ultimately brought researchers closer to the studied populations helped to break up the old register of persons, things and practices classified under the heading of Law.

Indeed, traces and hints of the abandonment of conventional legal dualisms can be found throughout Malinowski's oeuvre. For instance, he claimed that economic *exchange* has a ceremonial form like a ritual, and also defined *litigation* in terms of exchange (Malinowski 1926, p. 60). The clear definitions of economic and legal phenomena that can be easily identified in our own culture failed when applied in a different foreign setting. For the ethnographic observer, the legal boundaries and the boundaries between law and other cultural domains were blurred. This is certainly one reason why, as Moore put it, Malinowski "never abstracted legal principles altogether from the social context in which they occurred" (Moore 2000, p. 133), and also a reason why Malinowski himself claimed that "law and order arise out of the very processes which they govern" (Malinowski 1926, p. 123). Sometimes it was very difficult to distinguish between a sentence and an agreement (a *verdict* and a *contract*)—"in no case is there any definite sentence pronounced by a third party, and agreement is but seldom reached then and there" (Malinowski 1926, p. 60). However, the ethnographer's cognitive difficulty involved in differentiating law from other things should not be automatically imposed on the natives themselves, who did so without difficulty (see Malinowski 1926, p. 74). These blurred boundaries included not only cases of law and economics, but affected literally everything. For instance, the line between law and war was one of the most porous. Malinowski writes, "fighting, collective and organised, is a juridical mechanism for the adjustment of differences between the constituent groups of the same larger cultural unit" (Malinowski 1964, p. 261). It was only later that Pospíšil defined the line between law and feud using the distinction between intra- and inter-group behaviour (Pospíšil 1968). However, even such a demarcation should be understood as an analytical tool and not part of the real world. As we will see later in this chapter, the new ethnographic *modus operandi* became a *ratio operandi* for Malinowski's attempts at achieving a new understanding of law. Certain basic concepts of our culture such as "rules" were not simply directly applicable in foreign cultures, and "to a careful reader it soon became obvious that Malinowski's rule has little in common with abstract rules (written or memorized)" (Pospíšil 1974, p. 8). Also, for an analytical distinction between law intermingled with exchange and the complete separation between law and exchange in the form of scale (see Ledvinka 2012, pp. 56–59).

His natural inability as a non-native to discern law from other phenomena of social life "on the winding beaches and reefs" is perhaps demonstrated most radically in these two statements about law: "Law is the specific result of the configuration of obligations which makes it impossible for the native to shirk his responsibility without suffering for it in the future" (Malinowski 1926, p. 59), and: "The main province of law is in the social mechanism, which is to be found at the bottom of all the real obligations and covers a very vast portion of their custom, though by no means all of it, as we know" (Malinowski 1926, p. 62). These definitions should be interpreted neither to mean that authority (an equivalent to the Western court) is not a necessary attribute of law, nor that native law is exclusively some sort of "primitive international law" within which "self-help was therefore a normal procedure; in more serious cases, one can only appeal to one's kin, since one could not appeal to the Law or the State. Cases thus had to be settled ultimately by mutual agreement" (Singh Uberoi 1962, p. 7), which for Singh Uberoi means that "internal conflicts do exist (...) they are underground; and the Law, such as it is, knows them not" (1962, p. 85). Contrary to this deceptive interpretation, Malinowski was certainly well aware that the link between law and authority is very close and direct and that it could appear in significantly different forms. For example he was familiar with the work of his student Reo Fortune, *Sorcerers of Dobu* (1932), for which he wrote a preface and which he called "a triumph of the Functional Method" (1932, p. xviii). This student of Malinowski also wrote that "the other *tai sinabwadi*, big men, of the village took no part but listen quietly (...) for i *guguia*, he is laying down the law. There was complete silence, no reply or repartee, although obviously one or two persons and a small party of sympathisers were seething in revolt and being most severely tongue-lashed. Such a man as Alo can take risks in public admonishing. (...) Alo was the greatest magician – that is to say, governor and administrator of the native law" (Fortune 1932, pp. 83–85). Therefore, the later statement that "the principle of authority comes into being from the beginnings of humankind" (Malinowski 1944, p. 248) should not be seen as inconsistent with his previous thought, but as compatible with it. Although Malinowski's understanding of law develops over time, it should not be thus divided into stages, as was suggested by Edmund Leach (1957/1960), as his later ideas are fully consistent with his earlier views and his other thoughts.

Malinowski's theoretical answer to the cognitive dissonance between our categories of law and other domains of culture (both between and within), was as new as the thoroughness of the entire methodology based on participant observation. Malinowski chose to pursue an understanding of law that was somewhere between an excessively narrow, culturally determined definition of law (Hobhouse 1915; Tylor 1871) and an excessively broad, culturally deterministic definition (Lowie 1920; Hartland 1924; see Malinowski 1926, pp. 9–16). *Crime and Custom in Savage Society* described more than clearly that, in those instances of native relations when no authority is directly present, "legal machinery" (Malinowski 1926, pp. 54–55, 86) was understood as a combination of authority and other human agents, rituals and other supporting factors such as status artefacts, savage money, and mental objects as forces of magic (for a different view see, e.g., Pękala and Stępień 2012). This is completely misunderstood by critics of Malinowski's definition of law as overly inclusive, a criticism that was surely not based on a sympathetic reading. His appeal for understanding law in broader terms than just the courts and police does not automatically mean that we must consider "all the complicated and varying considerations of personal motivations" (Redfield 1967, p. 4). It is nevertheless true that later only Llewellyn, Hoebel and Pospíšil proposed a theoretical separation of law and custom as analytical categories, and that this aspect of the anthropological understanding of law was not a guiding feature of

Malinowski's work. But this failure can be considered a minor detail in his shifting of all legal thought from a juristic to an anthropological modus.

Malinowski demonstrated that *law* as observed in an exotic location no longer resides within fixed boundaries, within fortified domains built from the inside out by jurisprudence with "our" legal practices and materiality as an implicit backdrop, but that it can be rediscovered within a seamless web of associations with other aspects of the foreign culture. Malinowski and all anthropology of law that followed this line of research are thus situated in this dissonant ground between our own modern legal categories and those of native "jurists," as both of them are built from the inside out. As it approaches the law of the Other from the outside, the anthropology of law thus attempts to reconcile this direction of study with a theoretical understanding of law. The notion of "the existence of interconnected institutions" (Moore 2000, p. 11) thus seems to be a perfect tool for re-directing theoretical thinking about legal worlds. From this point of view, it is clear that the only scholars who see any inconsistencies in Malinowski's thinking about law are those who do not recognise that, within the foreign culture, law is situated within a seamless web, not pre-divided by modern legal dualisms. For example, in *Argonauts of the Western Pacific*, the deployment of the new methodology forced Malinowski to disrupt any direct linear connection between law and text, i.e., to deny the concept of law as something written. The older concern of ethnographic fieldwork had been to give the chaos of exotic social life a clear and firm scientific order. It preferred a "codification" of living knowledge, rather than trying to understand its dynamics. Because this older approach often confused law with the regularities of other foreign cultural phenomena, another decisive step by Malinowski (one that changed ethnography's method of inquiry and its relationship to power) was to disconnect law from code and text. But where Law could be found, if not in written laws. Malinowski answers bluntly: "these things, though crystallised and set, are nowhere formulated. There is no written or explicitly expressed code of laws, and their whole tribal tradition, the whole structure of their society, are embodied in the most elusive of all materials; the human being" (Malinowski 1922, pp. 10–11). That was a step from research as codification towards the study of sociocultural dynamics, which includes the legal dimension.

Malinowski was nevertheless fully aware that the researcher himself necessarily engages in some sort of codification during research. He also knew that the researcher might insert consistency or logic, and that it is not necessarily the same consistency that can be found in the native point of view (Malinowski 1922, p. 10). He definitely did not mean to pretend that native law is "a consistent body of rules", as William Seagle (1937) said of him. There was always an awareness that anthropological research can act as a transformative medium and that native law as a well-composed logical and consistent system may well be the "professional product" of the researcher (Moore 2000, p. 11). However, this awareness should not be understood as an argument for disputing the inherent logic and rationality of native legal systems. On the contrary, for the ethnographic observer it is the unknown logic (and its missing premises) that confuses him. In many cases, however, references to traditional and customary law within political struggles for independence can be read as a sort of cargo cult of modern law or its contra-culture, which might lead (and often does) to achieving politically independent legalities (see Ledvinka 2016).

In this vein, we may speculate that while the modifiers "social and cultural" (when applied to anthropology) indicate for Malinowski that an ethnographic field has not yet been divided up according to pre-existing modern propositions, Malinowski preferred the term "biological" over "natural" and "psychological" over "individual", probably because in certain cases the observed subject was too tightly bound to the standpoint of the observer, biologist or psychologist. Malinowski rejected rationality as a dividing line both between a rational law of nature (natural law) and an irrational law of culture (positive law) and between a rational law of culture (Western law) and an irrational law of nature (savage law). However, the rejection of rationality as a dividing line between modern law and the law of the Other has not left a vacuum. As I will demonstrate later, it was replaced by another factor—reciprocity. During Malinowski's time, anthropology was still playing an unfortunate role in European expansion by helping to transform the legal systems of the Other into static and controllable units for the purposes of administration and social control. Malinowski's approach "was not concerned with reconstructing the pre-contact social systems and cultures, nor was it concerned with policy and administration. Research was to focus on the temporary changes that were occurring (...) to understand better ways in which these are being affected by the new influences [and the—ed. T.L.] tendencies towards new grouping and the formation of new social bonds" (Chanock 2000, p. v). There was a clear shift from the standpoint of the observer to the standpoint of the observed.

4.5 Law and Science

As Malinowski used the method of participant observation in the context of a non-literate society, his anthropology had to treat law as a form of native knowledge, a sort of ethno-law. As with ethno-science, law proved itself to be a native tool as necessary for survival as navigation was for the *Argonauts*—and its shortcomings could be no less dangerous. Perhaps even more than navigation, the native law studied by Malinowski could be seen today as another form of lost knowledge that is vanishing along with the disappearing worlds of Melanesia and other remote cultures all around the world (see, e.g., White and Tengan 2001). This concept of law shifted from written statutes to applied knowledge resulting from the employment of intense personal fieldwork for studying law, and is very significant from the perspective of disciplinary histories. Before Malinowski, the legal and scientific dimension of non-modern cultures was not recognised or only semi-recognised; Durkheim and some other nineteenth-century thinkers established a link between magic and religion on the one hand and criminal and primitive law on the other hand as a proposition for the further study of those domains. The treatment of law as knowledge would have been seen as a huge divergence from this arrangement of norms and facts which strictly separated religious from secular and rational from irrational of the time. The complexity of ethno-law claimed by Malinowski thus significantly shook the proposition that (real) law—more specifically, civil law—was reserved for the West or the North, while custom was reserved for the South or East, just as science belonged to the West and magic to the rest of the world. There was a certain symmetry between the nineteenth-century ethnographic treatment of law and its treatment of science (e.g., Scott 2011), as both were considered rational and Western. Therefore, Malinowski was certainly aware of the necessity to take the same kind of approach to custom, law and social control as he had attempted with magic, science and religion (Malinowski 1948; Tambiah 1990). Because these areas are closely linked, they are difficult to identify in a foreign culture. Outlining each area's respective function should be represented as a kind of provisional trick for how to distinguish them during fieldwork, when the researcher was detached from the categories of his or her own culture (as they were not of any help in the field) but not yet sufficiently attached to the native point of view.

In this process there are at least two compatible but seemingly contradictory steps whose incomprehension can lead us astray, as happened to some researchers. First, Malinowski placed law on an equal footing with other areas of culture and society such as religion, economy and kinship etc., as, in his view, law also deserved an autonomous analytical category within anthropological theory. Second, he nevertheless realised that law should not be treated as a delicate, special or even privileged field of study that required an autonomous methodology that would be fundamentally separated from participant-observation methodology. Because law, like navigation, is native knowledge, it is nothing special and can be studied using the same methodology as any other area of social life. From the viewpoint of social science, law should not be interpreted exclusively by juristic theology, which can sometimes take the form of legal science or jurisprudence, for this juristic theology must be studied as a part of law just as religious studies researches both religions and their theologies. These two steps thus result in two detachments in our understanding of law: (1) from the juristic claim that "our law" is a privileged supra-empirical entity that can be studied only by jurisprudence and legal theory as a special scientific field, and (2) from the idea that the "law of the Other" is immersed in customs and other aspects of culture (analytically inseparable from non-legal normativity) such as magic or *kula*. Malinowski thus directed anthropologists towards examining the widely held belief that modern law is characterised by (secular) rationality. Precisely this practice, which describes other cultures' entire legal systems merely in terms of the sacred while ignoring much of their profane normativity, is thus implicitly abandoned. The practice was later conceptualised as "the danger of double selection" (Tambiah 1990, p. 92).

Among the Trobrianders, Malinowski thus found that law was distinct from other areas of life, but modern guideposts did not help with its identification there. At the same time, getting a picture of the native understanding of law was a desirable but almost utopian goal. The possibility of an anthropological approach that might be able to exist somewhere between "our" law and the law of the Other was based on two facts—there are no longer any uncontaminated native legal systems and the real problem is the transition between native and "modern" systems. Further, because native legal understanding contains bias just as much as our own juristic understanding, accepting it uncritically without anthropology to act as a mediator would only lead to the accumulation of legal biases, but not to an understanding of them. If Malinowski could live in one legal system and then effortlessly go to live in another, there would be no need for the social science of law. In reality this crossing between cultural and legal environments remains very difficult, especially when the differences are enormous. The act of moving from one legal system to another can feel brutal, drastic and inhumane (Malinowski 1926, pp. 94–98). For this reason, when studying law in the ethnographic field, it is necessary to work from a position between legal systems and disciplines.

4.6 Reciprocity as a Disconnecting Factor

One of Malinowski's tools for managing the anthropologist's sense of being in-between was the later frequently misunderstood concept of reciprocity. However, when reading through the half-dozen critics and interpreters of Malinowski, followed by a reading of his work on law itself, the reader cannot avoid but feel the sheer discrepancy between Malinowski's writing and that of his critics when it comes to the significance of reciprocity within law. Some of his critics use the concept of reciprocity as a weapon against Malinowski, claiming (wrongly) that he considered reciprocity the main attribute of law and that it is the foundation for his definition of law. Hoebel's criticism (1954, pp. 180–184), for example, condensates previous misconceptions (especially Seagle's) and provides heavily false picture of Malinowski's anthropology of law. His statements that Malinowski's fieldwork was "placid trip on the lagoon," that the role of reciprocity was exaggerated by Malinowski whereas sanction and coercive force was largely underestimated, or that primitive law was defined by Malinowski merely in terms of civil law and reciprocity, are simply incorrect. However, Hoebel's (1954) and Seagle's (1937) criticisms contain some inspiring moments, their main arguments against Malinowski are not anymore acceptable today. If we listen to Pospíšil, whose criticism is among the fairest, we encounter Malinowski's fallacy of "superrational behaviour," which meant that "the mechanism of reciprocity [itself] exercises control over the behaviour" (Pospíšil 1974, p. 30). Pospíšil's interpretation is explicitly founded on the postulate that Malinowski (1934, pp. 30–42) pursued "a single criterion of law that would constitute its essence" (Pospíšil 1974, pp. 29–30)—which he found in reciprocity. However, Malinowski neither offered an explicit definition of law that was connected directly and exclusively to reciprocity, nor did he hint at such a direct link. On the contrary, together with systematic incidence, publicity and ambition, reciprocity is considered to be only one of "the main factors in the binding machinery of primitive law" (Malinowski 1926, p. 68). If we were to be fair, in this vein we would have to say that, for example, ambition is a defining feature of law. But what would that mean?

The source of confusion in this critique is twofold. As Pospíšil expressed elsewhere, he was trying to find a workable analytical definition of law using a procedural rather than a substantive basis. It nevertheless remains unclear whether Malinowski related reciprocity to the procedural or substantive part of legal systems. It seems that the dividing line between those two areas was never without dispute. The second, and perhaps more important thing, is that reciprocity played an entirely different role in the definition of law than it did as the main attribute of law. It is associated with Malinowski's requirement to search not only for an equivalent to criminal law, but also for an equivalent to civil law within the seamless web of the native legal-cultural system, and thus to dramatically extend the scope of cross-cultural comparisons when compared to earlier ethnography. This extension helped to liberate the anthropological understanding of law from the fractured authenticity of earlier ethnography and resulted from a yearning for a more solidly founded analytical starting point. It is well known today that the early ethnography of the nineteenth and early twentieth century received ideological support and an organisational basis from colonialism (Nakai 1994, p. 22). Today, law (as divided into Savage and modern) is also widely recognised as having been a key factor in the era's European expansion (Haldar 2008, p. 4; Mommsen and de Moor 1992). In this context it was undesirable for early ethnographers to search for an equivalent to civil law or to even consider civil law comparable to "primitive" law.

Why? According to the doctrine of international law, sovereignty over territory considered *terra nullius* may be acquired through occupation. There is a corresponding doctrine of civil law that ownership over things which are *rēs nullius* may be acquired through appropriation. If we apply our archaeological imagination to travel into the past, we will find a time—certainly much earlier than the nineteenth or early twentieth century—when everything that is currently in some recognised form of ownership belonged to nobody, but this was not the case during the colonial era. The establishment of certain land as *terra nullius* (and thus also of the things within this land as *rēs nullius*) has always been a complicated long-term half-legal/half-scientific operation, based on findings that certainly differed enormously from the native point of view held by those who lived in this "no man's land". The desirable colonial description of a *terra nullius* would thus be a place with no equivalents to European civil law but whose legal system differs from European legal systems in certain fundamental respects. The limits of such an approach soon become clear, for anthropological descriptions of "archaic law" in the no man's land or in other targets of colonial desire were sometimes paradoxical. While early ethnographers were looking for an equivalent to Western criminal law, they found its counterpart: vengeance. To understand why vengeance as a mechanism of repression can be seen as a counterpart to Western criminal law, it should be noted that for a long time modern criminal law was exclusively dominated by the idea of crime as a breach of abstract order. The idea that a crime can be primarily understood as a breach of the relationship between perpetrator and victim came first with the recent return of the repressed (in Western legal science) concept of restorative justice and victims' rights, which has once more blurred the line between the civil and the criminal in modern culture (see, e.g., Visinger 2012).

The modus operandi of vengeance found by early ethnographers was based on reciprocity between the group (family, clan, sub-clan etc.) of the victim and the group of the perpetrator and struck them as essentially private. In many non-modern cultures, vengeance could even be avoided through the strange notion of *blood money*, which resembles a civil law institution much more than one from criminal law. In terms of modern law, it is analogous to applying compensation under civil law to cases of murder.

Whereas ethnographers and jurists can easily distinguish between criminal and civil legal institutions in their own culture, they are often very uncertain when doing so in a foreign context. The conventional way of distinguishing between civil and criminal law is to consider criminal law a rigid *ultima ratio* that sets the sinful individual against the sacred domain of *ordre public*, while in civil law it is primarily up to the parties to decide on the adequacy between the worth of each promise and the sanction for its breach. By comparison, the reciprocity found throughout the equivalents of the main branches of modern law in Trobriand society was a contributing factor to ethnographers' decision to no longer distinguish between civil law as reserved for moderns and criminal law as reserved for the "Savage". Similarly, the less famous concept of "publicity inherent in the structure of their society" (Malinowski 1926, p. 58) can be considered a hidden element in both public and private law, because its factual distribution throughout the various branches of law blurs the dividing lines found in Trobriand law and consequently in modern law as well.

If there is no direct link between law and reciprocity, should we not rather see reciprocity as an inter-group (and thus extra-legal) phenomenon that intensively influences the shape of intra-group legal rules and their enforcement? In fact, Malinowski speaks of reciprocity in this way as well: "Each community has therefore a weapon for the enforcement of its rights; reciprocity" (Malinowski 1926, p. 23). He also emphasises that law involves "a whole system of mutualities" and "chains of reciprocities". These indicators led us away from Pospíšil's understanding that reciprocity lies between two individuals. Although reciprocity may concern the individual obligations between persons from different communities, Malinowski pointed out that it is also a complex relation between communities and their legal systems. Although reciprocity is described as a "constraint" or "force" (Malinowski 1926, pp. 28, 29), there are some hints that, rather than being merely inter-individual, reciprocity is more appropriately considered both an inter-group and an inter-individual phenomenon. Reciprocity is also described as both "artificially, culturally created dependence" (Malinowski 1926, p. 28) and "the give-and-take principle" (Malinowski 1926, p. 47). Reciprocity thus cannot be considered a universal attribute of law; it is certainly not the factor that makes law legal. It can be embodied in law or re-established by law, and in some cases law can banish it as well. Hoebel assumed, in my view deceptively, the opposite opinion claiming that "[t]hey are all bound together in reciprocity. This makes it legal in Malinowski's view, for any undue chiselling by the one side will lead the other to withhold its services" (1954, p. 180).

4.7 The Conflict of Legal Systems and Malinowski's Unrecognised Discoveries

For a complex understanding of "law in Malinowski's terms" (Hoebel 1954, p. 180) it is necessary to consider how reciprocity is actually situated within inter-tribal relationships. If reading *about* Malinowski's views of law will soon set readers against him, a reading *of* Malinowski himself may come as a great surprise. Although the critical atmosphere surrounding Malinowski resulted from an aversion towards some of his most uncritical disciples—Hoebel called them "Malinowskiites"—and their more or less dogmatic adoption of his ideas—"Malinowskiism" (1951, p. 247)—he himself was mostly respected as an original thinker and sincere fieldworker. Nevertheless, we encounter both fair and unfair criticism. While Pospíšil's criticism is among the most fair, Seagle (1937) and Hoebel (1954) criticise Malinowski for ideas that he would never have agreed with. Hoebel's evaluation of Malinowski's *Crime and Custom in Savage Society* (1926) is a fine example: Hoebel claims that the first part of the book (on anthropological definitions of law) is "climaxed midway", while the subsequent last half of the book is "a patchwork of instances of disorders (...) that ruffle the idyllic reciprocal tranquillity of the islands" (1954, p. 182). In fact, the chapter on the definition of law is an attempt at linking the book's first part (which critically evaluated several older anthropological studies of law in the light of Malinowski's Trobriand fieldwork) with its last part on significant discoveries regarding Trobriand law.

By comparison, Pospíšil recognised Malinowski's ideas, alongside those of Otto von Gierke, Max Weber and several others, as a milestone on the road towards the anthropological theory of a multiplicity of legal systems (later known also as legal pluralism or the theory of legal levels). According to Pospíšil, Malinowski did not see the answer that was lying right under his nose: two parallel systems of law within one society. Pospíšil pointed out that "Malinowski also failed to conceptualise multiple legal systems within the same society and link them to the pertinent social structure" (Pospíšil 1974, p. 102). This criticism of Pospíšil is inspiring and incomplete at the same time. Malinowski was at least ready to recognise a multiplicity of legal systems, as is clear from his early writing in which he mentioned, for instance, that "the fifty-three states and territories with radically different legal systems and consequently different social problems offer an excellent field of observation and experimentation to the sociologist. The lack of religious, political and legal unity, and the partial lack of national unity, and their separation from historical tradition and routine, makes it possible to raise many questions about the practice of legislation" (2006, p. 265). Such a surprising understanding of American law fits perfectly into the later theory of the multiplicity of legal systems (Pospíšil 1971, pp. 97–126) and was a part of Malinowski's thinking even before he conducted his fieldwork on the Trobriands. The question thus is why Malinowski did not recognise the existence of multiple native legal systems when he was at least theoretically ready to see the possibility. The answer is simple. He in fact recognised it very explicitly: "The law of these natives consists on the contrary of a number of more or less independent systems, only partially adjusted to one another. . . [the systems] can also trespass beyond its legitimate boundaries" (Malinowski 1926, p. 100). Malinowski clearly saw "the law of these natives" as a configuration of "systems," except that not all of them were legal. Pospíšil's focus is thus on the degree of their legality, on a scale ranging from an absence of law to the existence of undepreciated law. I would nevertheless emphasise that the more important part of his criticism has remained unrecognised: It is true that Malinowski carelessly mixed together far too many small yet decisive scientific steps in a very short text. There is one thing that very much confused Malinowski. Some "classificatory rule" (Malinowski 1926, p. 113) preferred one legal system (Mother-Right) over another (Father-Love), thus leading him to the conclusion that one should be considered "strict law" and the other "legalised usage" (Malinowski 1926, pp. 121, 123). This was possible only because his thinking process was influenced by another factor—Malinowski used the distinction between legal ideal and sociological reality (the difference between abstract rule and the manner in which it is enforced) to explain the difference between the two legal systems. This difference can be described as a legality or illegality only if we adopt the *exclusive perspective* of one of the legal systems (that are present in the given situation) which does not recognise the legality of the other legal system(s).

As a result, it was not difficult to mistake the distinction between legal ideal and sociological reality for a distinction between two legal systems. However, neither Malinowski nor Pospíšil recognised that the discovery of "systems of law in conflict" (Malinowski 1926, p. 100) was much more complex, and that it had theoretical implications beyond the recognition of a multiplicity of legal systems. Malinowski namely provides us with an explanation of why he cared about a native equivalent of the distinctive branch of law, the private international law of the natives, which is useful in some respects: "The study of the mechanism of such conflicts between legal principles, whether overt or masked, is extremely instructive and it reveals to us the very nature of the social fabric in a primitive tribe" (Malinowski 1926, p. 100). Malinowski speaks about the "classificatory principle of kinship", which is distinct from both legal systems (called "Mother-Right" and "Father-Love") and which, along with Mother-Right, "is associated with the totemic system, by which all human beings fall into four clans, subdivided further into an irregular number of sub-clans" (Malinowski 1926, p. 113). Therefore, this principle does not directly belong to any of the mentioned legal systems; instead, "kinship" is an equivalent of the modern *connecting factor* (a concept found in the theory of private international law), which helps Trobriand legal authority to resolve the question of which legal system to apply to cases involving people from different Trobriand subgroups (for more details about modern connecting factors in conflict of laws, see, e.g. Currie 1959). This rare and specific kind of legal conflict, one that was more than just a common legal dispute among people from the same social group, attracted Malinowski's attention. As anthropologists usually acknowledge neither the domain of private international law in general nor its concept of connecting factors in particular, this is just to point out that the knowledge of this modern branch of law would help to truly understand

Malinowski's ethnographic conclusions about Trobriand law and the role of reciprocity within it. We cannot continue to neglect those discoveries by Malinowski just because they have not been widely intelligible among anthropologists. However, the issue goes even beyond social science as private international law's concepts (including reciprocity) are not notorieties even among non-specialised jurists. When Malinowski writes about the "law's perfection" (1926, p. 5) as a part of modern bias, he means that the idea of a single harmonic legal system prevented ethnographers from gaining an authentic understanding of native law—which, as Pospíšil recognised, was heterogeneous. Although Pospíšil identified two parallel legal systems in Malinowski's field, he overlooked several other aspects of the Trobriand legal enigma that I would like to point out here. First, it was eventually recognised that Malinowski explicitly wrote about three legal systems—two native and one European—not as a matter of comparison, but because they were all present in his ethnographic field. Second, they were in conflict with one another because of incompatible legal principles. Third, there were two types of solutions to these conflicts: either according to the "classificatory rule" or through "delegalisation". Although delegalisation of the law of the Other is in certain respects antithetical to the approach of private international law, which views legal systems as equals of sorts, it could be also be seen as a solution to the conflict between the legal principles of the Trobriand system and the modern system. Malinowski thus detected the Trobriand equivalent of modern private international law, as well as a way of escaping the fact that Trobriand legal systems really exist. There are thus two approaches to the problem of assimilating to a legal system other than the one that we grew up in: Spatial re-location and a voluntary ritual of transition from one to the other, on the one hand, and the mechanical application of our law onto foreign society, accompanied by the complete denial of the existence of native law, on the other. Whereas native legal systems contain "methodical systems of evasion" such as cross-cousin marriage (Malinowski 1926, p. 99, 110) that might reconcile individual personality with the shock of a legal transition, the European legal system does not admit (as a consequence of its denial of the law of the Other) that such a transition may be dramatic at all. Malinowski's point lies in the comparison between these two solutions to conflicting legal systems. He emphasises that an individual's transition from one Trobriand legal system to another is dramatic enough to result in *suicide*. Malinowski indeed perceived suicide by jumping from a palm tree as an attempt at escaping the implications of the law (Malinowski 1926, pp. 94–98). If this happens within a culture that we as outsiders view as homogenous, just imagine the disastrous impact of applying foreign laws onto native societies based on the assumption that they have no law (delegalisation).

While Malinowski described in detail the "classificatory rule" of the Trobrianders' "archaic" private international law, along with its consequences for the natives and for the unity of the clan (Malinowski 1926, p. 112), concluding that "unity exists on one side, but is combined on the other with a thorough-going differentiation" (Malinowski 1926, pp. 115–116), his description of the equivalent phenomenon in European law (Malinowski 1926, p. 106), which I have called delegalisation, is sheer and cryptic: "The rash, haphazard, unscientific application of our morals, laws, and customs to native societies, and the destruction of native law, quasi-legal machinery and instruments of power leads only to anarchy and moral atrophy and in the long run to the extinction of culture and race" (Malinowski 1926, p. 93). Thus, Malinowski's anthropology is not just "the science of the sense of humour" (2015, p. 301)—the comparative conclusion made it also the science of bitter irony, thus changing the meaning of the words in the title of his main "legal" book, *Crime and Custom in Savage Society*: whose crime and custom is it, and who defines it (European legal authorities or one of the Trobriand legal authorities). Is it not an act of complicity to assume that a particular society of Others has no law (or has only customs) if doing so leads to suicides, even if only as an unintentional consequence?

4.8 Cross-cultural Comparison as a By-product

Although Malinowski did not apply the early comparative approach, his focus on the conflict of legal systems implies that comparison was not entirely insignificant. Instead, it was re-assembled within ethnographic fieldwork and played significant role in defining law according to his terms. Primarily, Malinowski constantly and systematically tried to detach his readers from what he called "the trend of general bias" (Malinowski 1926, pp. 57–58), which could be read as an encrypted reference to the way in which careless ethnographers inserted modern legal dualisms into their observations or conclusions. As mentioned above, this trend was embodied by the "absolute rigidity of criminal law" and the "corresponding denial of the possibility of civil law" within the "comparative studies of law" (Malinowski 1926, pp. 57, 56). Although Malinowski considered criminal law to be "falsely connected with the problem of 'government' and 'central authority'" (Malinowski 1926, p. 66), contrary to Hoebel's claim that Malinowski had a "definite distaste for forces of social coercion" (Hoebel 1954, p. 181), this quote can only be interpreted to mean that Malinowski was calling for research into *not only* criminal law *but also* civil law equivalents. At the same time, he ensured that anthropology's internal expansion of intercultural comparisons onto other branches of law would go along with its external expansion onto all legal systems irrespective of their (religious, political, ethnical, economic etc.) qualities—i.e., including Trobriand law as well. This step had two implications. Because Malinowski made his comparison while partly situated within the native's social and cultural predicament, the primary message is that the anthropological comparison of legal systems cannot take place in a vacuum but stems from the context of law, as well as from what the ethnographer would define as law at first glance. The conflict of legal systems that Malinowski witnessed first-hand among the Trobrianders prevented him from ignoring these seemingly extra-legal realities in his theoretical considerations. The early comparativists, they were named by Malinowski (1926, pp. 2–3) himself: "Bachofen, Post, Bernhoft, Kohler and the other writers grouped round the

Zeitschrift fur vergleichende Rechtswissenschaft", who played an important role in establishing anthropology and comparative law, refrained from studying the conflict of legal principles. Even today conventional comparative-law scholars ignore the context of laws, which they treat as isolated units. For anthropologists, however, the treatment of legal systems as autonomous, comparable entities is a delusion, even if it this is how comparative lawyers actually work. Nevertheless, the autonomy of the compared legal units suggests that there is a great distance or an impervious border between them in the real world as well. Malinowski's study of the Trobriand legal microcosm demonstrated that at least this early comparative suggestion is highly misleading, and so his consideration of context changed what was being compared. Laws (in the strict sense of comparative law) were replaced by the problems into which the law had become embroiled, such as the nature of the Oedipus complex (1926, 1927), the contrast between the norms of sexual practice in the Trobriand Islands and in Europe (1929), and the application of foreign law (Trobriand and European) within different contexts (1926). Malinowski's comparison, however fragmentary, was not shallow. He studied the impact of foreign law both on the lives of individuals and on the unity of society. Clearly, the search for equivalents to modern branches of law in native culture and the problems of applying foreign laws to native populations are deeply interconnected. Malinowski was thus not far from making "cross-cultural comparisons for the public good" (Fox and Gingrich 2002, p. 3).

If the concept of reciprocity is seen as a disconnecting factor in liberating anthropological thought from the narrow scope of modern legal dualisms, it should be no surprise that Annette Weiner sees reciprocity as "a Western cultural construction" (1992, p. 17). Indeed, Malinowski's comparison was to certain degree one-directional and thus incomplete. He attempted to make the native law of the Trobriand Islands intelligible to Western academia, and the concepts of reciprocity, publicity, and civil or criminal law should be understood as points of reference for audiences located on one side of this comparison. It is nearly impossible to find an equivalent translation of modern law or legal thought for native peoples. Reciprocity should thus be seen not as a construct but rather as an empirical example of *similarity* (although unfortunately somewhat de-contextualised) that helped establish a comparative connection between modern law and the law of Others. Nevertheless, Malinowski's decontextualisation is acceptable if we consider the discipline's stage of development at the time. At the same time, however, it is necessary to conclude that whereas "the comparative method and ethnographic fieldwork in the classic structural-functional Malinowskian sense are traditionally seen as opposed to each other" (Peacock 2002, pp. 46–47), Malinowski himself freely intermingled the two. Comparison was neither suspect nor impossible for him, nor did he refrain from relying on the research of others. Whereas Nader claims that "he was not a comparativist; he let his ethnography speak about Us, more or less *implicit* observations, whether he wrote about law and order, magic, science, and religion, or sexuality" (Nader 2011, p. 214), it would be more precise to say that he was not an *early* comparativist. He differed from them radically because his comparisons, perhaps one of the most persuasive distinctive features of his anthropology, were synchronous and thus disconnected from evolutionary schemes. Such synchronous, problem-oriented intercultural comparisons clearly demonstrate that, whereas evolutionary theory requires comparative studies, anthropological comparisons do not require evolutionary models (cf., e.g., Wolf 2002, p. 116). The true difference between early comparisons and Malinowski's comparison was that Malinowski transformed comparison from a principal method into a principal conclusion of research. It was not the main stated aim of his ethnography, however, but rather a by-product. The tensions between ethnographic research conducted in a small community, although treated as a microcosm of a larger (e.g. Trobriand) cultural entity, and the risky procedure of intercultural comparison were neither unambiguously resolved in favour of the former, nor the later. The problem-oriented approach did not allow for such an escape; instead, intensive personal fieldwork "created a new object of ethnographic study, which might prove to be related to similar institutions elsewhere" (Kuper 2002, p. 161). In this vein, Marcel Mauss—building primarily also on *Argonauts of the Western Pacific*—created the most influential anthropological comparison ever written (1925).

However, Malinowski made contradictory statements about the relationship between reciprocity and Trobriand society. While "society is based on the principle of legal status," (Malinowski 1926, p. 46), "the division into totemic clans is characterized by reciprocity" (47). This could be considered a clear departure from Maine's theory that law developed from status to contract (1873). If this interpretation is correct, than native law could be a combination of both forms (legal status and exchange), thus refuting the evolutionary divide between law founded on status (archaic) and law founded on contract (modern). However, both status and reciprocity are things that "must be arranged." (Malinowski 1926, p. 46) The detachment from the categories, dualisms, dichotomies and binary oppositions found in juristic thinking could not be more complete.

4.9 Participant Observation and the Law of Natives

The character of the anthropologist, jurist, ethnographer or sociologist can hardly be considered as given. Instead, it must be constantly built up against the other academic identities, as their mutual differences are rather subtle. The disciplinary traditions share much in common, and thus what really matters is the configuration of those common elements and how they recast reality "through a mysterious transformation wrought by science" (Geertz 1967) into specific disciplinary outputs. For this reason it is necessary to be more careful when assessing Malinowski's place in time. As was mentioned above (in Sect. 4.3), Malinowski did not invent participant observation, but he placed this method before all others to form the core of anthropological methodology. This shift does not imply an absolute denial of other methodologies, but rather involves their reconfiguration—as with cross-cultural comparison, which newly appeared among the final research conclusions, or practices employed by comparative lawyers, which can be newly seen as a part of the ethnographic field embedded within the conflict of legal systems. These elements have not disappeared. They are simply not among the principal methods of social anthropology.

Nevertheless, it was participant observation that benefited Malinowski the most, not only "in spite of his personal torments or because of them" (Geertz 1967) but also because it removed him from the legal theories found in various disciplines at the time—not because their leading proponents were thousands of miles away, but because their theoretical confidence (which would have influenced Malinowski at home) was replaced by the empirical facts about law that Malinowski himself detected so relentlessly in the field. Not only did these empirical facts affect Malinowski's knowledge, but one might say that they also changed his character or identity. Such are the implications of applying the participant observation method. Geertz poses an important question in this respect; "'Truly', [Malinowski—ed. T.L.] says in the concluding sentence of the diary, 'I lack real character'. Perhaps; but it rather depends on what is meant by character" (Geertz 1967, p. 298). I would develop this idea further to suggest that personal character can also include legal identity (or rather, legal bias), which the ethnographer must overcome in the field.

Unfortunately this well-documented moment of transition from the normative attitude of earlier ethnography and legal theory towards the reflexive attitude of modern social and cultural anthropology has yet to be properly incorporated into our historical understanding of the evolution of the anthropology of law. Nevertheless, it is clear that the modern legal dualisms, which were a part of ethnographer's "home identity," were found to be inapplicable in the ethnographic field, and this was a direct result of the use of participant-observation methodologies that "were meant to allow the ethnographer to 'grasp the native's point of view, his relation to life, to realise his vision of the world'" (Nader 2011, p. 214). This method made the earlier normative confidence appear inauthentic because its schemes, postulates and propositions suddenly lacked any integrative central core in the new field of participant ethnography. It could be thus said that the abandonment of modern legal dualisms resulted in the partial loss of the ethnographer's original "home character", that the character did not pass the test of applying the participant observation method. Nevertheless, this "loss" must be considered an inevitable price for "underscoring the scientificity of ethnography by outlining three methodological tenets of research: (. . .) attention to the imponderabilia of actual life and observed behaviour, and the recording of spoken statements indicating the mentality of native thought" (Nader 2011, p. 214).

Ethnographers had some difficulty handling this moment in the evolution of anthropological studies. They felt it as a tragic failure and continued to take the self-doubt generated by the disparity between theoretical beliefs and new empirical facts to the extreme, without noticing that this moment could be understood as a "zero-point", a true opportunity for the researcher to develop an entirely new disciplinary character by learning how to operate in a constantly changing and unpredictable environment, in a situation of constant cognitive dissonance. The footing that might save anthropology can be found in a cross-disciplinary or diachronic comparison with the disciplinary past before the use of participant observation. The introduction of this method had a progressive impact on the configuration of self-doubt. Before, the legal or anthropological scholar's self-doubt was concerned with the correspondence between the real world and his theoretical armchair thinking, but with Malinowski self-doubt was related to finding a "rapport" between the native's point of view and that of the ethnographer when both are in the same place at the same time, in the field. Sometimes, this leads to absurd situations in which an ethnographer questions participant observation as an "illusion" because he or she is not "fully equipped with the native eye" (Nakai 1994, pp. 25–27). Such extreme soul-searching appears absurd when contrasted with today's eminent legal scholars who never even imagined the possibility of a dissonance between legal dualisms and the outside legal world. Nor do they ever consider the relationship between legal science's confidence and its proximity to the views held within the centre of power. For research in this field, see for instance the concepts of state science and nomad science in Deleuze and Guattari (2010, p. 19). While ethnographers realise that there is practically no such thing as an "uncontaminated native", most jurists have never read a single ethnographic or anthropological account about themselves over the ethnographer's shoulder. Although it is primarily the textual discipline of jurisprudence that goes back and forth between reading and writing, it is in fact ethnography that is concerned with the alleged predominance of writing over fieldwork. A cross-disciplinary comparison between social and legal science would thus provide some footing for those who are anthropologists only from within. The anthropology of law also developed from the moment when anthropologists lost their original theoretical confidence by broadening the temporal and spatial limits for normative diversity. This was a small but decisive step, in which Malinowski played important part, and anthropology gathered a mass of new knowledge that generated empirically-based certainty, however limited in scope. Therefore, it makes no sense to understand the loss of the original dualistic identity as a failure and to use this view as a weapon for undermining the established authority of anthropology, for this opens the door to comparatively antiquated disciplines whose confidence comes rather from the low degree of self-doubt resulting from their greater isolation from the field (or its inaccessibility via conventional methods). The empirical authority of anthropology, the Malinowskian "I" of the participant observer, is a demanding but utterly desirable ideal in comparison with other disciplines' methods. From the perspective of cross-disciplinary comparison it can be hardly seen as a ghost of the colonial past. It is its clear opposite.

4.10 Conclusion

Firstly, I suggested that Malinowski be seen as a disciplinary Other, as it would diminish his significance to see him merely as a quasi-jurist. It was later found that although Malinowski was truly a disciplinary Other, different from legal scholars, he was more practically oriented than most jurists. His coordination of rigorous social science with cultural sensitivity brought very practical results. His research pointed out that the strict application of knowledge claiming to be universal or global can have drastic impacts without further knowledge of the specific context in which the conflict between legal systems takes place. Second, I proposed that several lines of research have been inspired wholly or in part by Malinowski's legal anthropology because he established law as an autonomous field of study (although one that was interconnected with other parts of culture) and because he insisted that even the official law of developed countries must be studied using the same methodology as the one he applied in his study of Trobriand legal systems. Third, I suggested that this new methodology based on participant observation helped to liberate anthropology from the categories and dichotomies associated with modern legal dualisms, for they cannot be applied in a situation where the researcher sees law as contained within the seamless web of the foreign culture. Fourth, I proposed that anthropologists take seriously Malinowski's suggestion that the distribution of law between the West and the rest must be treated in the same way as science, because they are both situated in the same way within Western cosmology as tokens of rationality. Fifth, I suggested detaching the concept of reciprocity from Malinowski's definition of law, because however significant it may be (as suggested implicitly by Malinowski himself) it is just one principle among many. Reciprocity as a defining attribute of civil law played another role in liberating anthropology from an excessively narrow understanding of law, but as a *legal* principle it was not too broad to affect the average person (to use an inappropriate legal metaphor). It helped to extend the scope of commensurability in the way that Savage law can contain equivalents to all branches of modern law (albeit differently distributed), and made it possible to compare both European law with Trobriand law, i.e., with any non-modern legal system. Sixth, the relationship between suicide and the conflict of laws was used to emphasise the significance of Malinowski's still unrecognised discoveries related to native legal systems and their conflicting mutual relations, especially the "private international law of the natives", which is related to three different legal orders at least. Instead of being opposites, in Malinowski's study of law, ethnographic fieldwork and cross-cultural comparison were reassembled as a principal method and a principal research result. Seventh, participant observation was seen as a method capable of studying not only the cultural and social aspects of native law, but also the native legal systems themselves and their mutual conflicts, in which reciprocity played an important part. This was found as Malinowski's unrecognised starting point for the study of native legal dynamics, which helped him to avoid engaging in the codification that would freeze native "customs".

While studying the law of "disappearing worlds", Malinowski aimed to completely break free from the original division between normativity and facticity to master an entirely new discipline—an anthropology that would also study native law alongside the other domains of the foreign culture. Through his study of foreign cultures from Mailu to Kiriwina, he helped to establish another unique, no less exotic culture: the disciplinary culture of social and cultural anthropology, equipped to operate in spite of cognitive dissonances between differing normativities. The legal sciences of modern states could take this point into consideration and try once again to examine their own discipline's (academic) norms instead of forcing Malinowski's ideas on law back into the rigid framework of legal dualisms, which was clearly the tendency of several of Malinowski's critics. At the very least, by learning anthropology as a foreign language jurists could free themselves from their legal and disciplinary bias. In addition, instead of translating their own juristic or legalistic language into that of the anthropologist or vice versa, it would be more useful for them to realise that the Malinowskian anthropological study of law can illuminate possible links between local or specific legal practices, institutions or artefacts and the general objective knowledge of legal sciences, which are usually obfuscated by the way legal theory intermingles those local and specific legal elements into an abstract, universalistic and apodictic language of legal science. This is not an easy task, for it has become clear that to travel with Malinowski may provide many of different experiences, but it will be far from a "placid trip" into "the idyllic reciprocal tranquillity of the islands".

References

Abel, R. (ed.). 1982. *The politics of informal justice*. New York: Academic Press.

Bohannan, P. 1957. *Justice and judgment among the Tiv*. London, New York: Oxford University Press.

Bohannan, P. 1967. Differing realms of the law. In *Law and warfare: Studies in the anthropology of conflict*, ed. Paul Bohannan, 43–50. Austin: University of Texas Press.

Chanock, M. 2000. New introduction. In *Law as process: An anthropological approach*, ed. Sally Moore, 1–31. Münster: LIT Verlag Münster.

Conley, J., and W. O'Barr. 1990. *Rules versus relationships: The ethnography of legal discourse*. Chicago: University of Chicago Press.

Conley, J., and W. O'Barr. 1997. Crime and custom in corporate society: A cultural perspective on corporate misconduct. *Law and Contemporary Problems* 60: 5–22.

Currie, B. 1959. Notes on methods and objectives in conflict of laws. *Duke Law Journal* 2: 171–181.

Deleuze, G., and F. Guattari. 2010. *Nomadology: The war machine*. Seattle: Wormwood Distribution.

Donovan, J., and H.E. Anderson III. 2003. *Anthropology & law*, 2003. New York: Berghan Books.

Engelund, H. 2015. Law, law everywhere. *Hau: Journal of Ethnographic Theory* 5(3): 267–271.

Fortune, R. 1932/2013. Sorcerers of Dobu: The social anthropology of the Dobu Islanders of the Western Pacific. London: Routledge.

Fox, R., and A. Gingrich. 2002. Introduction. In *Anthropology, by comparison*, ed. R.G. Fox and A. Gingrich, 1–24. London: Routledge.

French, R. 1995. *The Golden Yoke: The legal cosmology of Buddhist Tibet*. Ithaca: Cornell University Press.
Geertz, C. 1967. Under the mosquito net. *The New York Review of Books* 9(4): September 14.
Gluckmann, M. 1955. *The Judicial Process among the Barotse of Northern Rhodesia*. Manchester: Manchester University Press.
Gluckmann, M. 2012. *Politics, law and ritual in tribal society*. Chicago: Aldine Transaction.
Greenhouse, C., B. Yngvesson, and D. Engel. 1994. *Law and community in three American towns*. Ithaca: Cornell University Press.
Haldar, P. 2008. *Law, orientalism and postcolonialism: The jurisdiction of the Lotus-Eaters*. London: Routledge-Cavendish.
Hartland, E. 1924. *Primitive law*. London: Methuen & Co. ltd.
Hobhouse, L. 1915. *Morals in evolution: A study in comparative ethics*. New York: H. Holt.
Hoebel, E. 1951. Review of Ralph Piddington, an introduction to social anthropology (Volume One). *American Anthropologist* 53(2): 246–248.
Hoebel, E. 1954. *The law of primitive man: A study in comparative legal dynamics*. Cambridge: Harvard University Press.
Hoebel, E. 1967. Law-ways of the Comanche Indians. In *Law and warfare: Studies in the anthropology of conflict*, ed. P. Bohannan, 183–294. Austin: University of Texas Press.
Hutchins, E. 1979. Reasoning in Trobriand discourse. *The Quarterly Newsletter of the Laboratory of Comparative Human Cognition* 1(2):13–26.
Hutchins, E. 1980. *Culture and inference*. Cambridge: Harvard University Press.
Josselin de Jong, J. 1948. Customary law: A confusing fiction. *Koninklijke Vereeniging Indisch Institut* 80(29): 3–8.
Kuper, A. 2002. Comparison and contextualization: Reflections on South Africa. In *Anthropology, by comparison*, ed. R.G. Fox and A. Gingrich, 143–166. London: Routledge.
Latour, B. 2002. *La fabrique du droit. Une ethnographie du Conseil d'État*. Paris: La Découverte.
Leach, E. 1957/1960. The epistemological background to Malinowski's Empiricism. In *Man and culture: An evaluation of the work of Bronislaw Malinowski*, ed. R. Firth, 119–138. London: Routledge & Kegan Paul Limited.
Ledvinka, T. 2012. Cultural determination of jurisprudence and the anthropology of law. In *Towards an anthropology of the legal field: Critiques and case studies*, ed. T. Ledvinka, K. Varhanik-Wildova, et al., 50–63. Prague: Fakulta Humanitních Studií Univerzity Karlovy v Praze.
Ledvinka, T. 2016. Subaltern law: Legal technology of making the law of the other. In *Non-humans in social science*, vol. 3, ed. M. Stella, P. Gibas, K. Pauknerova. Cerveny Kostelec: Pavel Mervart.
Llewellyn, K., and E. Hoebel. 1941. *The Cheyenne way: Conflict and case law in primitive jurisprudence*. Norman: University of Oklahoma Press.
Lowie, R. 1920. *Primitive society*. New York: Boni and Liveright.
Macaulay, S. 1963. Non-contractual relations in business. *American Sociological Review* 28(1): 55–67.
Macaulay, S. 1995. Crime and custom in business society. *Journal of Law and Society* 22: 248–258.
Maine, H. 1873. *Ancient law: Its connection with the early history of society and its relation to modern ideas*. London: Henry Holt & Co.
Malinowski, B. 1922. *Argonauts of the Western Pacific: An account of native enterprise and adventure in the Archipelagos of Melanesian New Guinea*. London: Routledge and Kegan Paul.
Malinowski, B. 1926. *Crime and custom in savage society*. New York: Harcourt, Brace & Co.
Malinowski, B. 1927. *Sex and repression in savage society*. London: Kegan Paul, Trench, Trubner & Co.

Malinowski, B. 1929. *An ethnographic account of courtship, marriage, and family life among the natives of the Trobriand Islands, British New Guinea*. New York: Eugenics Pub. Co.. *The Sexual Life of Savages in North-Western Melanesia.*

Malinowski, B. 1932/2013. Preface. In *Sorcerers of Dobu: The social anthropology of the Dobu Islanders of the Western Pacific*, ed. R. Fortune, xvii–xxx. London: Routledge.

Malinowski, B. 1934/1961. Introduction. In *Law and order in Polynesia*, ed. H. I. Hogbin, xvii–xxii. Hamden: The Shoe String Press.

Malinowski, B. 1935. *Coral gardens and their magic*. London: Allen & Unwin.

Malinowski, B. 1944. *Freedom and civilisation*. New York: Roy Publishers.

Malinowski, B. 1948. *Magic, science and religion and other essays*. Boston: Beacon Press.

Malinowski, B. 1964. An anthropological analysis of war. In *War: Studies from psychology, sociology, anthropology*, ed. L. Bramson and G.W. Goethals, 245–268. New York: Basic Books.

Malinowski, B. 2006. *The early writings of Bronislaw*, Malinowski ed. R. J. Thornton and P. Skalnik. Cambridge: Cambridge University Press.

Malinowski, B. 2015. Anthropology is the science of the sense of humour: An introduction to Julius Lips' *The savage hits back, or the white man through native*. *Hau: Journal of Ethnographic Theory* 5(3): 301–303.

Mauss, M. 1925/1973. Essai sur le don. Forme et raison de l'échange dans les sociétés archaïques. In *Sociologie et Anthropologie*, ed. M. Mauss, 149–279. Paris: Presses Universitaires de France.

Mommsen, T., and J.A. de Moor. 1992. *European expansion and law: The encounter of European and indigenous law in 19th- and 20th-century Africa and Asia*. Oxford, New York: Berg.

Moore, S. 2000. *Law as process: An anthropological approach*. Münster: LIT Verlag Münster.

Nader, L. 1990. *Harmony ideology: Justice and control in a Zapotec mountain village*. Stanford: Stanford University Press.

Nader, L. 2011. Ethnography as theory. *Hau: Journal of Ethnographic Theory* 1(1): 211–219.

Nakai, A. 1994. The ethnographic unconscious: Malinowski and the Freudian text. 大学院英文学研究会,リーディング. 第14号 (10):22–35.

Offner, J. 1983. *Law and politics in Aztec Texcoco*. Cambridge, New York: Cambridge University Press.

Peacock, J. 2002. Action comparison: Efforts towards a global and comparative yet local and active anthropology. In *Anthropology, by comparison*, ed. R.G. Fox and A. Gingrich, 44–69. London: Routledge.

Pękala, M., and M. Stępień. 2012. The relation between law and magic: Preliminary remarks. In *Towards an anthropology of the legal field: Critiques and case studies*, ed. T. Ledvinka, K. Varhanik-Wildova, et al., 24–34. Prague: Fakulta Humanitních Studií Univerzity Karlovy v Praze.

Pospíšil, L. 1958. *Kapauku Papuans and their Law*. New Haven: Yale University Press.

Pospíšil, L. 1968. Feud. In *The international encyclopaedia of the social sciences*, ed. D.L. Sills and R.K. Merton, 390–392. New York: The MacMillan Company and the Free Press.

Pospíšil, L. 1971/1974. *Anthropology of law. A comparative theory*. New York: Harper and Row.

Pospíšil, L. 1973. E. Adamson Hoebel and the anthropology of law. *Law & Society Review* 7(4): 537–560.

Redfield, R. 1948. Introduction. In *Magic, science and religion, and other essays*, ed. B. Malinowski, vii–xi. Boston: Beacon Press.

Redfield, R. 1967. Introduction. In *Law and warfare: Studies in the anthropology of conflict*, ed. P. Bohannan, 2–16. Austin: University of Texas Press.

Riles, A. 2011. *Collateral knowledge: Legal reasoning in the global financial markets*. London: University of Chicago Press.

Rosen, L. 1989. *The anthropology of justice: Law as culture in Islamic society*. New York, Cambridge: Cambridge University Press.

Schapera, I. 1957/1960. Malinowski's theories of law. In *Man and culture: An evaluation of the work of Bronislaw Malinowski*, ed. R. Firth, 139–156. London: Routledge & Kegan Paul Limited.
Scott, C. 2011. Science for the West, myth for the rest? In *The postcolonial science and technology studies reader*, ed. S.G. Harding, 175–197. Durham: Duke University Press.
Seagle, W. 1937. Primitive law and Professor Malinowski. *American Anthropologist* 39(2): 275–290.
Singh Uberoi, J.P. 1962. *Politics of the Kula Ring: An analysis of the findings of Bronislaw Malinowski*. Manchester: Manchester University Press.
Starr, J. 1992. *Law as metaphor: From Islamic courts to the palace of justice*. Albany: State University of New York Press.
Tambiah, S. 1990. *Magic, science and religion and the scope of rationality*. Cambridge: Cambridge University Press.
Tylor, E. 1871. *Primitive culture: Researches into the development of mythology, philosophy, religion, art, and custom*. London: J. Murray.
Visinger, R. 2012. Anthropological legitimisation of restorative justice. In *Towards an anthropology of the legal field: Critiques and case studies*, ed. T. Ledvinka, K. Varhanik-Wildova, et al., 35–49. Prague: Fakulta Humanitních Studií Univerzity Karlovy v Praze.
Weiner, A. 1992. *Inalienable possessions: The paradox of keeping-while-giving*. Berkeley: University of California Press.
White, G., and Tu Kâwika Tengan. 2001. Disappearing worlds: Anthropology and cultural studies in Hawai'i and the Pacific. *Contemporary Pacific* 13(2): 381–414.
Wolf, J. 2002. Conditions of comparison: A consideration of two anthropological traditions in the Netherlands. In *Anthropology by comparison*, ed. R.G. Fox and A. Gingrich, 95–123. London: Routledge.
Yan, T. 1995. Fictio legis: L'empire de la fiction romaine et ses limites médiévales. *Droits* 21 (July): 17–63.

Chapter 5
Reciprocity as a Species of Fairness: Completing Malinowski's Theory of Law

James M. Donovan

5.1 Introduction

Bronislaw Malinowski is rightly revered for laying the foundations of a modern anthropology based on extended fieldwork conducted in the local language while sharing the daily living circumstances of the hosting group. His work paved the way for the discipline's theoretical reorientation away from a collection of bizarre and foreign customs among so-called "primitive" groups, and toward a search for the underlying similarity shared by all humans whatever the technological status. While over his career Malinowski would pursue these themes in a variety of sociocultural contexts including magic, religion, and economics, his initial efforts found a fruitful context in the relationship between law and society.

The problem of law touched immediately upon the errors he hoped to correct in the style of anthropology practiced by his contemporaries. Armchair speculators such as E. Sidney Hartland voiced the opinion that indigenous folk (variously labeled "savage" or "primitive") lacked law, and were instead organized and motivated by a visceral adherence to custom (Hartland 1924, p. 138). While Hartland was largely correct that local peoples do not always employ the same conceptual categories to demarcate the kinds of social activities in which they engage (e.g., they "draw no line between law and morality, religion, medicine, or art"), he then leapt to the unwarranted conclusion that they therefore lack those activities as we would recognize them. Having no separate category of "law" was taken as proof that law as we define it did not exist. Swimming in an indistinguishable stew of custom, the "primitives" exist literally in a permanent condition of lawlessness, and, by extension, immorality and probable criminality.

J.M. Donovan (✉)
College of Law, University of Kentucky, Lexington, KY, USA
e-mail: james.donovan@uky.edu

M. Stępień (ed.), *Bronislaw Malinowski's Concept of Law*,
DOI 10.1007/978-3-319-42025-7_5

This view marks not a mere mistake of fact, but more, an oppressive assertion concerning the kinds of beings that are these "savages". Under this reading "primitives" are categorically different from the modern European, requiring a separate psychology and exemption from the standard account of what constitutes "human nature" and therefore human society. Not only does this position get the science wrong, but it also provides warrant for colonial adventuring justified with a banner of bringing civilization, i.e., "the law," to the childlike "savages".

Throughout his career, Malinowski attempted to rebut this image of the local peoples as qualitatively different from the Western European. Although never satisfied with his solutions, he consistently strove to characterize law as an institution of social regulation shared by all human groups. The challenge for this project was to describe law in a manner that would convince the reader that law indeed was being talked about even when lacking "central authority, codes, courts and constables" (Malinowski 1926, p. 14). While his attempt to identify reciprocity as the underlying motive of law seemed initially productive, the rudimentary understanding of reciprocity available to him resulted in the failure of this line of inquiry.

The present essay seeks to recast Malinowski's arguments grounding law in the social phenomena of reciprocity in light of current information. Reciprocity is argued to be a higher order construct built out of more basic influences, the most relevant of which are the inherent fairness evaluations humans perform in contexts of distributive justice. Deconstructing Malinowski's claims into these elemental components preserves the original insight that explains the civil law in terms of social reciprocity. More importantly, this analysis generates a description for the criminal law in these same terms, something Malinowski himself was unable to achieve. The outcome realizes his goal of providing a coherent account of law as a cross-cultural human universal.

5.2 *Crime and Custom* and the Limits of Reciprocity

Malinowski's most influential writing on the question of law and society, and the one that arguably chartered the specialty of legal anthropology, appeared in his 1926 classic, *Crime and Custom in Savage Society*. In this brief monograph Malinowski employed two analytic strategies. First, he distinguished civil from criminal law, and second, he explained the former, but not the latter, as emerging organically out of social reciprocity. Although these arguments touch on genuine insights, as applied they do not yield the theoretical benefit Malinowski intended.

5.2.1 Two Kinds of Law: Civil and Criminal

Distinguishing between the civil law and the criminal law was not an original strategy. The division is recognized by the Western legal tradition against which

Malinowski wrote. The criteria he employed to demarcate the two forms, however, are unique. In Malinowski's formulation, civil law is the normal social condition, "the law obeyed", while criminal law is "the law broken".

The divide Malinowski marked overlaps one of methodological discernment. Identification of the civil laws, the ones obeyed, relies upon a normative, statistical claim that, on average, a person in that situation behaves according to the rule. Patriarchal societies follow patrilocal marriage customs, for example. Exceptions exist, but on the whole, the group's ideal mode and often its typical pattern conform to this expectation. Criminal law, on the other hand, is noticed in the breach, in what Llewellyn and Hoebel (1941) would later term the "trouble cases". Civil law is an ideal constructed out of prescriptive statements about how people *ought* to act, while criminal law flows from a realist's observations about how people *actually* behave. From this perspective the two kinds of law are incommensurable and cannot be easily combined into a generic "law", forcing Malinowski to treat them separately.

This outcome, however, undermines his goal to offer an account for "law" generally. For Malinowski the primary challenge was to bring together these legal rules. Before considering Malinowski's efforts, we should recognize the concerns as to whether, in spite of its popularity in the West, the distinction as drawn is valid from any view. Despite the difficulties they raise, Malinowski's categories can be judged superior to the alternative versions found in the literature.

For example, in some lines of jurisprudence the differentiating quality between civil and criminal law looks to the locus of the injury. Crimes threaten the welfare of the group and provoke a broad social reaction; merely civil concerns address disputes between individuals without ordinarily threatening the general cohesion of society at large.

While conceptually attractive, this approach relies upon a difference in degree rather than kind, a criticism common to all the alternatives here reviewed. Instances of such blurring include murder, the prototypical criminal act, often understood to threaten society because unconstrained internal violence can unravel the bonds holding the group together. Yet in earlier times murder could be regarded not as a public offense, but as a private wrong to be avenged by the victim's family (e.g., Gagarin 1986, p. 89). Traces of the personal interest in murder remain in the ability for families to pursue civil actions against a murderer beyond the state criminal proceedings, as famously seen in the case against footballer O.J. Simpson (Ayres 1997).

A second alternative distinguishes civil and criminal law by the kinds of punishments to which the defendant is vulnerable. While the full menu of penalties are in play for criminal infractions—fines, prison, execution—only the first is available for civil suits. Here we again see the problem of sorting consistency. Although debt is today a prototypical civil issue, not only has debt collection resulted in imprisonment in the Dickensian past, but jail time for failure to pay remains a possibility. While some of these cases involve nonpayment of fines associated with criminal charges (Cal. Pen. Code § 1205(a)), others concern instances of ordinary private liabilities such as inability to pay child support (Brunker 2011; Texas Appleseed 2014).

Especially problematic with this characterization of the criminal/civil divide is the ethnographic fact that, as thus defined, the criminal law often collapses into the civil law. Cross-culturally, imprisonment is not always an option. That limitation means that, unless the imposed penalty is death, this typology offers an uncertain basis on which to differentiate criminal from civil violations. Attempts to employ kinds of punishments as a distinguishing feature in contexts where not all options are available can result in unwarranted characterizations of those legal systems as either lacking a criminal law, or perhaps being more draconian, more "barbaric", than our own for always resorting to the death penalty. Posner (1985) noted this tendency for pre-modern societies to rely heavily upon capital punishment, but rather than dismiss this pattern by disparaging the groups he explains the trend as a rational response to a need to deter deviant actions paired with a low probability of capture.

However defined, the recognition of two disparate kinds of law, the civil and the criminal, remains a problematic assumption. In the end, civil law is what is labeled as the civil law, and likewise for the criminal law. Treatment of socially constructed categories as natural kinds inevitably introduces complicating premises into any work of general theory such as Malinowski hoped to offer. The ambiguity of the definitional criteria leads to indeterminate boundaries between the contrasted categories that may not accommodate the differing accounts of the two kinds of law. Concepts that shade gradually from one into the next may be a convenience for code builders, but they cannot support a characterization of the difference in kind that is usually required to defend the formal bifurcation of legal forms.

For these and other reasons, anthropologists have become skeptical about the benefits of speaking in terms of a divide between the civil and criminal laws outside the cultural and historical context in which those types originally emerged. Radcliffe-Brown observed the "confusion which has resulted in the attempt to apply to preliterate societies the modern distinction between criminal law and civil law" (Radcliffe-Brown 1952, p. 212), and Nader (2002, p. 8) suggests that "the existence of different native categories of law forces us to question the two powerful categories of Western law—'civil' and 'criminal'—as cultural constructs that are the legacy of a specific Western lawyering tradition".

These objections notwithstanding, the fact remains that many writers do find the distinction between the criminal and the civil law to be meaningful and helpful. Malinowski was too deliberate a scholar to fall thoughtlessly into the established categories. We may therefore question why Malinowski chose to make this typology the basis of his argument, especially as the decision will prove an impediment to his broader purposes. Two suggestions shed possible light on this puzzle. First, Malinowski was motivated to respond to the discourse about the law as it stood, and which denigrated local populations. That discussion was frequently cast in these dyadic terms, making it reasonable that he would follow the same pattern. Perhaps more importantly, by separating the acts of group cooperation from those of individual deviance, Malinowski could create a suitable context in which to isolate what he believed was the underlying psychological mechanism leading inevitably to the formation of legal institutions: reciprocity.

5.2.2 Reciprocity as the Fount of Law

Within *Crime and Custom* Malinowski differentiated civil and criminal law in one additional way to which he does not draw our attention, but which further complicates the account. Drawing upon his observations of the network of relationships necessary to build a canoe (described fully in *Argonauts of the Western Pacific* [Malinowski 1922]), Malinowski (1926, p. 20) extrapolated to find "a rigid system of mutual obligations, into which a sense of duty and the recognition of co-operation enter side by side with a realization of self-interest, privileges and benefits". Generalizing this motive, he named this thread connecting individuals into a cohesive whole of society to be "reciprocity". Reciprocity provides the phenomenological experience of law as a binding obligation that he believed separates law from mere custom.

The argument below builds upon this identification of reciprocity as fulfilling a uniquely seminal role in the creation of legal institutions. Given that prominence, it may be worthwhile to briefly consider a different view, one that "there is no direct link between law and reciprocity" within Malinowski's writings. As offered in this volume's contribution by Tomas Ledvinka, reciprocity is only one of many imaginable components of law, none of which is necessary or sufficient. His textual warrant is Malinowski's summary claim that "reciprocity, systematic incidence, publicity and ambition will be found to be the main factors in the binding machinery of primitive law" (Malinowski 1926, p. 67). As he reads the statement, reciprocity is only one of several variables that may or may not be found in legal systems.

Even if we concede that actual legal systems will often display traces of the qualities in that list, Ledvinka misses the especially close relationship between reciprocity and at least the civil law within the argument. Malinowski stated plainly that

> 'Civil law', the positive law governing all the phases of tribal life, consists then of a body of binding obligations, regarded as a right by one party and acknowledged as a duty by the other, kept in force by a specific mechanism of reciprocity and publicity inherent in the structure of their society (Malinowski 1926, p. 58).

Malinowski used the term "publicity" only one other time in the book—the penultimate page—so we do not know what he meant by the term or whether it adds anything new to the idea of reciprocity. We are entitled to take Malinowski at his word and echo his claim that reciprocity is an inseparable element of (again, at least) the civil law. One cannot fairly read Malinowski without recognizing the special importance he placed upon reciprocity for the institutions of law.

While informative on many points, Ledvinka's hermeneutic method understates the constraints of the problem Malinowski strove to solve in the short chapters of *Crime and Custom*, to rebut the pervasive and condescending depictions of "primitives" as lacking law. To reach that result, Malinowski must convincingly carve out a portion of social interactions from other normative relationships that critics already recognized, such as religion and custom. He required a rational ground to support his claim to study what others believed did not exist, law among "savages". Simple assertion is inadequate; the challenge is to demonstrate that of necessity law must exist given the kind of thing that groups are. This is the unique work Malinowski assigned to reciprocity. Because reciprocity is "inherent in the structure of society", it is able to perform this work as an originating source for legal institutions in a way that idiosyncratic facets of personal psychology, like ambition, cannot.

An account of law that finds its raw material in the reciprocal relationships within all groups resolves longstanding jurisprudential debates. Grounded in the universal human need to cooperate to survive, Malinowski's model allows all human societies to have something that can be recognized as "law" even when lacking the specific accoutrements familiar from Western institutions. Earlier theorists such as Locke had characterized law as something humans might achieve subsequent to their original condition. Against this background in which legal institutions are an uncertain social achievement, Malinowski's argument is that law flows inevitably from the fundamental realities of group living, that it is intrinsic to social organization and not an optional possibility enjoyed by some but unrealized by others: "Law represents rather an aspect of their tribal life, one side of their structure, than any independent, self-contained social arrangements" (Malinowski 1926, p. 59). In a later work Malinowski makes more explicit the basis of this argument:

> Every cultural activity again is carried out through co-operation. This means that man has to obey rules of conduct: life in common, which is essential to co-operation, means sacrifices and joint effort, the harnessing of individual contributions and work to a common end, and the distribution of the results according to traditional claims. Life in close co-operation—that is, propinquity—offers temptations as regards sex and property. Co-operation implies leadership, authority, and hierarchy, and these, primitive or civilized, introduce the strain of competitive vanity and rivalries in ambition. The rules of conduct which define duty and privilege, harness concupiscences and jealousies, and lay down the charter of the family, municipality, tribe, and of every co-operative group, must therefore not only be known in every society, but they must be sanctioned—that is, provided with means of effective enforcement (Malinowski 1939, p. 949).

To be human is to live in cooperative groups, which entails the presence of legal forms.

Malinowski concluded the book's first section on civil law with the well-known statement that:

> There must be in all societies a class of rules too practical to be backed up by religious sanctions, too burdensome to be left to mere goodwill, too personally vital to individuals to be enforced by any abstract agency. This is the domain of legal rules, and I venture to

> foretell that reciprocity, systematic incidence, publicity and ambition will be found to be the main factors in the binding machinery of primitive law (Malinowski 1926, p. 67).

Malinowski proved to be a poor fortuneteller. While the reader tends to be satisfied with the argument thus far, a difficulty arises when we move to the book's second section on the criminal law. Although reciprocity serves as the basis for his provocative description of the civil law, it is nowhere mentioned in the subsequent pages. While the account of civil law built upon the cooperative activity of canoe building, the criminal law analysis begins with a suicide provoked by public accusation of a violation of the rules of totemic clan exogamy—the "law broken". This discussion was perhaps unsatisfying even to Malinowski, leading him to admit that the "'criminal' aspect of law in savage communities is perhaps vaguer than the 'civil' one" (Malinowski 1926, p. 94).

We should clarify what is at stake here. If criminal law cannot be explained by reciprocity, or by some structurally similar element that is equally "inherent in the structure" of societies, Malinowski cannot argue that criminal law is culturally universal in the same way he had just achieved for civil law. Lacking such proofs, he cannot refute those who would insist that these societies lack a criminal "law", and instead punish out of simple vengeance, blind custom, or heated anger.

Although not the direction in which Malinowski went, one might attempt to salvage the text by entertaining the suggestion that negative reciprocity could provide the connecting theme. If negative reciprocity is appropriate in this context, both forms of law could then fall under a single master concept. Unfortunately, serious difficulties prevent this saving reading of the text.

While reciprocity generally refers to the idea of returning good for good, negative reciprocity is the return of bad for bad. This is the "tit-for-tat" argument, in which we return what we have received, be it good or evil. When taking the form of criminal punishment, negative reciprocity at first blush allows both civil and criminal law to be described with a single motive.

This stratagem falters because, despite surface resemblances, reciprocity and tit-for-tat represent different ideas. Reciprocity is an open ended, forward-looking behavior from the perspective of the current gift recipient who typically views herself as the midpoint of a dynamic three-way exchange: what she first received, what she now gives, and what she anticipates receiving later in return. Tit-for-tat, however, describes a backwards looking conclusion viewing only two steps, the current one reacting to a prior act anticipating no additional interactions. It is retaliation intended to terminate an interaction, unlike the other's sympathetic gesture functioning to perpetuate the relationship. Beyond these structural differences, two additional factors undermine the possibility that tit-for-tat could be employed as the criminal law version of reciprocity—the moral/semantic and the empirical/economic.

For the first, reciprocity, according to one of the fuller discussions of the concept, refers to a moral obligation to "return good for good, in proportion to what we receive; [to—ed. J.D.] resist evil, but not do evil in return; [and to] make reparation for the harm we do" (Becker 1986, p. 4). By these terms, to the extent that criminal law entails the idea of punishment (by which we broadly mean the infliction of an undesirable penalty) it contradicts the underlying virtue usually in mind when discussing reciprocity. Reciprocity being the kind of thing that it is, it cannot be inverted to return bad for bad. Even when construed to mean no more than tit-for-tat, something Becker (1986, p. 94) and Kolm (2008, pp. 89–93) expressly preclude, if the punishment is a return for a crime (and not, for example, a consequence) then it is arguably an equally moral evil.

> Moral evil, under the general conception, is conduct (or its consequences) that is unjustifiable all-things-considered. It is, by definition, precisely what we ought not to do. So whether we have suffered evil or not, it would be self-contradictory (under the general conception) to recommend unjustifiable conduct. Reciprocity, if it is to be a moral virtue, cannot dispose us to act unjustifiably – to return evil for evil (Becker 1986, pp. 94–95).

We need not rely upon the characterization of reciprocity as a moral virtue to reach this result. The same cautionary outcome is attained when focusing only on the exchange component of returning like for like. Just as reciprocity builds relationships and rewards cooperation, negative reciprocity penalizes the defector through a tit-for-tat retaliation. Applying reciprocity in this manner to the analysis of criminal law will be effective only if tit-for-tat generates lasting social institutions of the kind Malinowski hoped to describe. Game theory experimentation, however, suggests that, outside dyadic interactions, tit-for-tat results in sustainable cooperative relationships only in very constrained conditions, "if the group is small, the returns to cooperation are high, the behavior of each group member is known with a high degree of accuracy by all of the other group members, errors in execution are infrequent, and group members are very patient and interactions typically endure for many periods" (Bowles and Gintis 2011, p. 64). This list of required limitations makes it unlikely that tit-for-tat can serve as a satisfactory general explanation for group cooperation, and for a social institution of punitive criminal law particularly.

Falling into this same category of the exchange or economic perspective, we can imagine that many deem the punishment received for a criminal act as in some nontrivial sense the price for the deviance, and thus something owed to the actor. The penalty serves, claims the Christian Bible, as "the wages of sin" (Rom. 6:23). Reciprocity, however, incurs no such overt and mundane debt. Indeed, great pains are made to avoid any appearance of merely discharging an obligation when offering a return gift. The recipient may deserve a gift, but he cannot claim it, in the way we speak of punishment as a debt that is owed.

Unintended endorsements of the claim that criminal law escapes the operations of reciprocity can be found. In their summary of this section of *Crime and Custom*, Conley and O'Barr (2002, p. 869) insert the idea of reciprocity where they think it belongs: a crime is "an act that (1) violates a fundamental social norm, (2) is not deterred by the ordinary incentives of reciprocity, (3) is made public, and (4) because of these other attributes, cannot be either ignored or resolved between individuals". Bringing the two into close proximity, however, underscores their inherent incompatibility: The criminal law is invoked when reciprocity fails, which requires that it be grounded in something else. If civil law follows upon reciprocity, criminal law is the absence of reciprocity. Rather than both kinds of law springing from a single cause, they become inversely related.

In sum, tit-for-tat and reciprocity are qualitatively different kinds of exchange relationships, and do not simply mark that one involves a trade in pains and the other in goods. The categorical semantic boundaries and the empirical limitations of tit-for-tat together suggest that negative reciprocity in the context of criminal law is not a simple or direct extension of the role of reciprocity in civil law. Something more will be required if we wish all of law to brought under the conceptual umbrella of reciprocity.

Perhaps for these reasons Malinowski remained unsatisfied with the outcome of *Crime and Custom*. He would continue to tinker with the elements of his theory relating law and society. Just a few years later, for example, he eliminated the divide between civil and criminal law and spoke only of a unitary category of law. Reciprocity remained an important explanatory principle, but now it had been paired with Austinian sanction and assigned a different function. Where earlier the psychological motivation of reciprocal benefits had been sufficient to create the binding obligation of (at least the civil) law, now it worked equally with the fear of sanction. In other words, he had mixed what in *Crime and Custom* were two distinct motivations into one, in the process diminishing the scope of reciprocity and returning the basis of law to one grounded on fear of punishment (Malinowski 1934). These changes put his revised formulation in line with others such as Weber (1954), but failed to be an improvement upon his earlier attempt not least because fear cannot adequately capture the ordinary experience of the obligation to obey the law (Tyler 2006), a priority lesson of *Crime and Custom*.

In many ways these changes were necessary corrections to the weaknesses of the 1926 essay, but they came at a high cost. These later versions no longer shielded indigenous societies from the charge of lacking law and thus left them vulnerable to "help [from—ed. J.D.] the white man to govern, exploit, and 'improve' the native" (Malinowski 1926, p. xi). Law was no longer a cultural universal; Malinowski (1934, p. xxv) is forced to concede, using the words of Radcliffe-Brown, that "some simple societies have no law".

He would in time turn away from this revision in one of his last published works (Malinowski 1942), suggesting that even in his own mind the solution to the problem had eluded him. His ongoing efforts to reshape the theoretical pieces of *Crime and Custom* into a workable model reveal his intuition that the short essay contained a spark of insight, but one that he could not hammer into a convincing theory (Donovan 2013, pp. 19–22).

The obstacle to forging a unified theory of law, I shall argue, is that Malinowski worked with the inappropriate unit of analysis by speaking in terms of the psychological motivations of reciprocity. When analyzed into its more fundamental concepts reciprocity may yet be the key to solving the problems Malinowski articulated. The hoped-for outcome is that the advances Malinowski offered in *Crime and Custom* can be preserved while avoiding the shortcomings he encountered in larger model-building.

5.3 Reciprocity and Fairness

Despite its shortcomings, *Crime and Custom* remains attractive for offering an intuitively appealing account of law that, unlike those offered by social contract theorists, understands law to emerge inevitably from the realities of group life. Given how characterizations of some groups as "lawless" have justified exercises of colonial expansion and cultural hegemony, a conclusion that all functioning human societies have law would be one worth preserving. More to the point, however, the work that law is expected to perform seems to be necessary to any well-functioning society whatever the technological level. Lacking resort to special definitional pleading that elevates certain cultures above others—as when Schiavone (2002, p. 3) argues that only those societies descended from the Romans can claim to have true law, or Tamanaha's (1993, p. 212) assumption that "law" refers only to "the law of the state", effectively excluding most of the world's traditional societies—the kind of thing that law is should be expected to appear everywhere much like religion, language, and kinship systems. In the presence of a viable account explaining such universal distribution, the burden of rebuttal shifts to the exceptionalists.

The challenge in crafting that account is to retain the beneficial insights of Malinowski's groundbreaking arguments while correcting its structural limitations. The previous section demonstrated that the largest of those shortcomings is an inability for reciprocity to account for both civil and criminal law. Whether this failing is insurmountable depends in part on whether reciprocity is what Becker terms "a fundamental virtue". Fundamental virtues are those which are: (1) deontic in character, referring to one's duties and obligations; (2) have a connection to other primary goods which are necessary for living; and (3) inclusive and relevant to a "wide range of activities and institutions" (Becker 1986, pp. 147–148). Becker (1986, p. 149) concludes that reciprocity, satisfying all three criteria, is not only a fundamental virtue, but "one of the *most* fundamental virtues – that in fact its only serious competitor for sole possession of the title is justice".

Missing is any requirement that a fundamental virtue be irreducible to more basic virtues. Fundamental does not mean elemental. To the contrary Becker (1986, p. 73) admits that reciprocity is "connected (both in theory and in practice) to prudence, self-interest, altruism, basic human needs, social welfare, notions of desert and duty, justice and fairness". He concedes that for at least some of these the relationship is not merely correlational, but rather compositional: "when the notions of fairness and fair play are explicated, their similarity to elements of the reciprocity disposition is unmistakable" (Becker 1986, p. 268). Fairness is not merely a homolog of reciprocity, it is constitutive of that concept.

For Becker, then, reciprocity can be analyzed into further components, the most important for our purposes being fairness. This section expands upon this observation through two specific claims. First, fairness considerations are not merely one facet of a larger reciprocity gestalt, but represent the element without which the relationship would fail to qualify as a reciprocity-based exchange. Second, fairness evaluations at the root of reciprocal exchanges are grounded in our biological natures, suggesting that while the forms and standards may be determined by local variables, the exercise itself is a human universal. The final section uses these results to construct a fairness-based interpretation of reciprocity. This revised statement of Malinowski's thesis resolves the identified shortcomings of his own original attempt to describe fundamental legal norms while preserving its conclusion that law is a cross-cultural universal.

5.3.1 Reciprocity as Fair Exchange

Malinowski's effort to employ reciprocity as the principle factor in the generation of law, although successful in the description of civil law, failed in the instance of criminal law. The difficulty may have been that reciprocity represents a complex concept. If it can be broken down into more basic features, then these may prove more effective units from which to build a general institution of law.

Within *Crime and Custom* Malinowski took reciprocity primarily as a given social fact to be described rather than a phenomenon to be analyzed. In the second chapter of the monograph he reviewed how the networks of mutual obligations had led earlier commentators to the mistaken conclusion that "primitive" groups operated under the premise of communal ownership of property such as canoes. On the contrary, drawing upon his extensive personal knowledge of the Trobriand society Malinowski (1926, p. 20) found that there exists "a definite system of division of functions and a rigid system of mutual obligations, into which a sense of duty and the recognition of the need of co-operation enter side by side with a realization of self-interest, privileges and benefits".

More specifically, Malinowski proceeded through a series of examples and arrived at the conclusion that the transactions typical of each such relationship, whether between individuals, communities, or some other bifurcated social division, contain "a sociological dualism: two parties who exchange services and functions, each watching over the measure of fulfillment and the fairness of conduct of the other.... In this and in all the manifold activities of economic order, the social behavior of the natives is based on a well-assessed give-and-take, always mentally ticked off and in the long run balanced" (Malinowski 1926, p. 26). Behavioral reciprocity, then, emerges from a background of assessed values between gifts received and gifts given.

Further details on the matter are to be found in Malinowski's earlier, more detailed ethnography presented in *Argonauts of the Western Pacific* (1922). Here the building of canoes is but one facet of a more extensive description of the Kula exchanges to which only passing reference is made in *Crime and Custom*. In the Kula, shell ornaments circulate in a ritualized pattern requiring long and treacherous sea voyages.

> The main principle underlying the regulations of actual exchange is that the Kula consists in the bestowing of a ceremonial gift, which has to be repaid by an equivalent counter-gift after a lapse of time, be it a few hours or even minutes, though sometimes as much as a year or more may elapse between payments (Malinowski 1922, p. 95).

Despite the important rule that the return gift be of equal value, this evaluation is wholly in the hands of the giver.

> The second very important principle is that the equivalence of the counter-gift is left to the giver, and it cannot be enforced by any kind of coercion. A partner who has received a Kula gift is expected to give back fair and full value, that is, to give as good an arm-shell as the necklace he receives, or vice versa. . . . If the article given as counter-gift is not equivalent, the recipient will be disappointed and angry, but he has no direct means of redress, no means of coercing his partner, or of putting an end to the whole transaction (Malinowski 1922, p. 96).

What prevents defection is the high cultural value placed not on the retention of wealth (as might be argued for our own society), but rather upon the distribution of wealth in acts of generosity. Deviations from a cultural norm of equitable return may be more the rule than the exception (Sahlins 1972, p. 127), but they can be tolerated because the embedding institution places the current inequity in a rolling context of overall fairness and ultimate appropriate balance.

We thus see that underlying Malinowski's characterization of reciprocity lurks an attention to the "fairness", "equivalence," and "balance" of the net merit of the exchanges of services and goods. His model of reciprocity highlights the cohesive outcome of mutual obligations grounded in iterated exchanges carefully monitored for their equitable merits, an outline we find echoed in other works.

Kolm's (2008, p. 11) theoretical summary of the theory of reciprocity parses the concept as springing from three distinguishable motivations: "a duty of social balance or equity, the interaction of liking, and a mutuality of interests". Of these, the first is arguably the most basic. Yunxiang Yan's ethnographic account of gift-giving in a Chinese village documents how, even when primarily motivated by the latter two of Kolm's impulses, the exchange never veers too far from considerations of the equitability of the gift: "one must know what kinds of gifts are suitable for which categories of relatives or friends . . . [because while the drawbacks of giving too little are easily seen, even—ed. J.D.] 'an unusually large gift could crush a person to death'" (Yan 1996, pp. 125, 127). Yan relates the story of a young man who, wanting to show his generosity after a successful move to the city, offered a wedding gift three times the normal amount. The gift, instead of earning the donor praise and gratitude, required that his parents apologize for their son's "improper conduct." Attention to equitable and appropriate gift giving is not idiosyncratic to this Chinese village. According to the latest edition of *Emily Post's Etiquette* (2011, p. 364), "Receiving an overly expensive gift from anyone other than a significant other or close family member puts the recipient in an awkward position. It becomes a lopsided relationship and the receiver can feel either owing or owned". Successful participation within a network of reciprocal exchanges requires sensitivity to the balanced merits of the flowing gifts, so that one gives and expects neither too little nor too much.

If, as Kolm (2008, pp. 15, 14) suggests, every "peaceful and free society" is "motivated largely by sentiments of reciprocity", then the fairness evaluations that make reciprocity possible are themselves enabling conditions for human communities (Mauss 1967). While a complete account of actual reciprocal networks such as the one studied by Yan will consider other influences— "personal interest, empathy, affection and liking, the values of being liked and the dynamics of mutual liking, responsibility, information and communication, interpersonal comparison resulting in status fairness, merit a sense of retributive and compensatory justice, moral indebtedness, a sense of propriety and duty, guilt or shame, an imitation and emotional contagion" (Kolm 2008, p. 17)—the elaborated concept is rooted fundamentally in an underlying ability to "keep score". Reciprocal exchanges may be more than fair exchanges, but they are always at least that.

Fairness should not be construed as insisting upon equality. Indeed, Malinowski appears to overstate the expectation that the return be equal, as opposed to the more flexible requirement that it be only equitable. While some ethnographic accounts may emphasize that the value of the gifts be equal, the broader rule is that the exchange be deemed acceptable to both parties. This may require that the gifts be unequal in absolute terms, but perhaps equivalent relatively (e.g., as a function of one's ability to give, or as related to status differentials as when Yan describes newly married couples staying outside the exchange networks until their families are established). In this sense, at least, reciprocity is built upon those fairness evaluations, and depends upon that ongoing calculation to qualify as what we would recognize as reciprocity.

Both Malinowski's cursory analysis and fuller contemporary descriptions converge on the view that the complex social behavior glossed as "reciprocity" grows out of an underlying ability to track social values and to compare them on a common metric to ascertain whether a subsequent gift is a fair return for an original offering. Claims about reciprocity, such as those made by Malinowski, may therefore be reframed in the more basic terms of fairness.

5.3.2 Innate Fairness Evaluations

Deconstructing reciprocity into claims about fairness does not immediately render the latter an effective theoretical substitute for reciprocity. The same parochialism that led many to believe that indigenous peoples lack law can also lead them to deny non-Western societies any interest in fairness on the grounds that they are insensitive to such virtues (e.g., Leslie 1879, p. 39). An argument must therefore be offered that the fairness perceptions underlying social reciprocity come naturally to all humans. This can be achieved through a demonstration that ascertaining equitable treatment is a general interest we share with other animal species, but one which also bears the imprint of cultural modeling. It is, therefore, both universal and particular, much like reciprocity itself.

5.3.2.1 Fairness Grounded in Human Evolutionary History and Developmental Psychology

In a *Nature* letter, Brosnan and de Waal (2003) reported the results of an experiment in which capuchin monkeys were differently rewarded for a standard task. While most were given cucumber slices, when a monkey witnessed a partner receiving the greater reward of grapes for equal effort, it ceased to comply with the task. The negative reaction became more marked if the partner was rewarded for no effort at all. This reaction was observed in female subjects, but not males, a pattern of gender difference in sharing behaviors also found among humans (Andreoni and Vesterlund 2001). A later study (Brosnan et al. 2006) replicated these basic patterns using chimpanzees, although the results were more complexly related to other variables such as group size, social closeness, and within-group traditions. The authors concluded that "these reactions support an early evolutionary origin of inequity aversion" (Brosnan and de Waal 2003, p. 297).

Research into nonhuman recognition of inequitable situations is a recent project. Not all are persuaded that the experiments support the scientists' suggestions that primate behaviors can provide insight into the evolutionary precursors of human mental processes. Stępień (2010) reviews the contrary arguments, and concludes that "some traits (empathy, sense of fairness) that might seem to be good candidates for having evolved as an adaptation (homology or analogy) may, on further and deeper examination, turn out to be rather poor candidates." Two replies respond to his concerns and will allow us to proceed under the premise that the roots of fairness evaluations reach far into human evolutionary history.

First, just as species-typical biological traits are expected to have an evolutionary history reflected in common ancestors, the same assumption has been defended for psychological traits. The field of evolutionary psychology has as one of its central tenets that "behaviors or traits that occur universally in all cultures are good candidates for evolutionary adaptations" (Schacter et al. 2009, p. 27) and recent work has proven this theoretical stance to be productive (e.g., Buss 2014; Cosmides and Tooby 2013). Any conclusion that a panhuman instinct for inequity aversion reflects a sui generis trait, one unique to our species, would be surprising in light of available ethological data (e.g., Cheney and Seyfarth 1990; Griffith 2001), and thus carries a high burden of proof. As noted by de Waal, "It's just inconceivable that perspective-taking and self-awareness evolved in a single jump in a few species without any stepping stones in other animals" (de Waal 2009, p. 139).

Second, the interpretive caution that Stępień advises primarily concerns the attribution of morality to nonhuman primates. The present discussion argues only that species other than *Homo sapiens* make calculations about material benefits and respond when finding themselves on the deficit side of the comparison. This observation entails no further conclusions about nonhuman morality than do descriptions of their sexual behavior. Because it limits itself to accounts of processes and the presumed underlying mechanisms that produce those results, without venturing onto the more problematic considerations of what values those might reflect, the present discussion thus seems to avoid the brunt of Stępień's critique. We are not here arguing that nonhumans are moral agents but only that they, like ourselves, are economic calculators of a rudimentary kind.

Granting that Brosnan and de Waal are justified in their conclusions that some nonhuman primates display an aversion to inequitable material rewards, a broader review of the literature demonstrates how widely across the genera this tendency appears. In addition to studies on the higher primates, similar results have been found in tamarin monkeys (Hauser et al. 2003), lower mammals such as canines (Beckoff 2004), and among some birds (Heinrich 1999). In her summary of this field, Brosnan (2006) describes perhaps the earliest formal work on the topic, Tinklepaugh's (1928) study involving macaques. When expecting a reward of lettuce, the subjects were happy to accept the snack; when expecting banana slices, but receiving only lettuce, the monkeys reacted with angry sulking. Such differential responses suggest that the animals did indeed have expectations that, when frustrated, provoked a negative emotional outburst, a social sanction of the feeder's apparent stinginess.

This ability to represent mentally an anticipated future event and compare it to the actual outcome is a preliminary step toward Brosnan's (2006) three-stage model of the evolutionary precursors of *disadvantageous inequity aversion*, "the tendency to turn down a perfectly good offer if others are getting a better deal" (Barash 2010). First is "the recognition that other individuals obtain rewards that are different from one's own," which involves substituting Tinklepaugh's one-subject comparison of states with a two-subject comparison of contemporaneous outcomes.

> At the second level, the maligned individual reacts to this discrepancy, which requires that the individual feel strongly enough about the discrepancy to alter their behavior. At the third level is the willingness to sacrifice in order to punish a lucky individual (Brosnan 2006, p. 161).

A fourth and final stage occurs when these three stages of increased sensitivity to equity disadvantage results in the individual becoming aware when she has been treated *better* than her peers. Related studies (Jensen et al. 2006; Silk et al. 2005) suggest that chimpanzees, despite their evolutionary proximity to humans, have not advanced further than step three, and it is not altogether clear that most people regularly achieve the fourth developmental stage. In an analysis of disputing parties in employment discrimination cases (Berrey et al. 2012), both sides expressed a conviction that "discrimination law is rife with unfairness, but each party points to unfairness in those aspects of the legal system that most disadvantage that party" while overlooking how the system may favor one's own position at the expense of the other's. The Internet meme to "check your privilege" can serve to remind "a person who is making a political point that they should remember they are speaking from a privileged position, because they are, for example, white, male, heterosexual, able-bodied or wealthy" (Freeman 2013), and thus likely to take for granted the advantages they enjoy in society.

The lesson appears to be that "our instances of 'unfairness' seem to be much clearer, sharper, and more concrete than the more abstract, aerial notions of 'fairness'" (Finkel 2001, p. xiii). The visceral awareness of unfairness precedes, and is the foundation from which our more rational formulations of justice, and self-conscious reflections on what is fair, emerge (Wolgast 1987). Thus, while discussions (including this one) label the phenomenon as "fairness", in point of fact we are often speaking instead of the contrary, of unfairness. Subjects are not truly calculating what is "fair", they are ascertaining whether the events are, from their perspective, "unfair". In most instances this changes little about the specific argument, but it is a fact that should be kept in mind nonetheless.

The data on the ultimate evolutionary foundation for fairness calculations can be paired with research on the proximate developmental patterns. Children behave similarly to the primates described, being "sensitive to inequality. . .but it seems to upset them only when they themselves are the ones getting less" (Bloom 2013, p. 80; see also LoBue et al. 2011). Bloom's survey of research on children too young to be merely mimicking learned behaviors leads him to conclude that "babies are moral animals, equipped by evolution with empathy and compassion, the capacity to judge the actions of others, and even some rudimentary understanding of justice and fairness" (Bloom 2013, p. 218).

Taken together, the ethological, ethnological, and human developmental studies overwhelming point to the conclusion that the ability to notice an inequitable distribution of resources is deeply rooted in the evolutionary histories of cooperative species, including *Homo sapiens*. "The reaction of children to perceived unfairness shows how deeply seated these sentiments are, and the egalitarianism of hunter-gatherers suggests its long history" (de Waal 2009, p. 184). If, as earlier argued, fairness constitutes the *sine qua non* of reciprocal exchanges, then reciprocity is presumptively also a human universal. We are, in the words of Pfaff (2007, p. 206), "wired for reciprocity".

5.3.2.2 Cultural Fairness Evaluations Both Universal and Specific

For an instinct for fairness evaluations to serve as a theoretical substrate for reciprocity, the former should cover the same scope and range as the latter, although the converse need not be true. As a more basic phenomenon, fairness calculations may occur without coalescing into full reciprocity, as it does among nonhumans; on the other hand, reciprocity cannot appear except out of fairness considerations.

The universality of reciprocity may appear to argue too much to the extent that it suggests that the form it assumes is also shared across all human societies. On the contrary, the norms of reciprocity will reflect the local understanding of what it means for something to be "fair". For that reason, while the previous section demonstrated that fairness evaluations, like reciprocal exchanges, are a human universal and thus display the required breadth, we must also argue that, like reciprocity, fairness assumes a bounded spectrum of forms incorporating the emphases of each particular society. Fairness, in other words, must be culturally universal in principle, but culturally specific in application; although humans innately invoke the idea of fairness (or unfairness), that concept is "never immutable, universal, or transcendent" (Berrey et al. 2012, p. 7), but is instead constructed locally.

The technique to map expectations concerning resource distribution problems involves experimental games, the most important of which is the Ultimatum Game [UG]. First described by Werner Güth in 1982 (McCabe 2003), the UG assigns two players to a noniterative exchange. From a set amount the first player makes an offer to an unknown second player, who decides to accept the offer, or to refuse it, in which case neither player keeps their portions. The game was devised to test the standard model of economic rationality predicting that the second player will accept any tendered offer no matter how low because something is always better than nothing. This expectation, however, has been repeatedly violated as players proved willing to incur a personal loss to punish someone who makes an offer that is judged too low, and thereby unfair. Although irrational from the perspective of rational choice theory, this behavior makes excellent sense in light of social psychology.

Using versions of the Ultimatum Game, fieldworkers have demonstrated that fairness determinations are present in all societies, and also that, while the results show cultural variability, "this variation correlates with differences in patterns of interaction found in everyday life" rather than with individual variations among subjects (Henrich et al. 2004, p. 5). For example, Brian Paciotti and his teammates characterized the different game strategies of two Tanzanian ethnic groups, the Sukuma and the Pimbwe.

> The Sukuma made hyperfair offers—more than half of the money. The Pimbwe respondents proposed significantly less—only 430 [out of 1,000] shillings on average in one within-village test and just 150 shillings in the between-villages test (Paciotti et al. 2005, pp. 58, 62).

This between-group difference was used to explain why only one group, the Sukuma, had succeeded in the rapid creation of "the highly cooperative and aggressive Sungusungu [an organization created to fight back against armed incursions from Uganda and cattle rustling—ed. J.D.]," which "grew from a grass-roots venture in a few villages in northern Tanzania to a successful justice system replicated and enthusiastically embraced by Sukuma communities across the country". Efforts by the Pimbwe to form a similar self-defense organization consistently failed, despite being motivated by the same obvious benefits. The authors theorize that, as the game had revealed, the "Sukuma—unlike other ethnic groups in Tanzania—already had rules that promoted large-scale trust, and they could quickly invent a justice system when the need arose".

The touchstone research on the cross-cultural comparison of fairness standards was conducted by a group led by Joseph Henrich. Together they played a variety of games within fifteen small-scale societies, producing results that support the conclusion that the range of behaviors judged to be fair is much more variable across cultures than originally believed. Compared with reports in the literature that most frequently sampled university populations, and which described offers that were "consistently 50 percent", within these non-Western societies "modes vary from

15 to 50 percent" (Henrich et al. 2004, p. 19). These contrasts do need to be read with caution, however. Even within modern societies there can be cultural differences concerning unfairness. Finkel (2001, p. 258) found that although "Japanese and Americans perceive the same major categories of unfairness (...) their salience differs by culture". The Western/non-Western contrast may thus be an artifact of our available data. The Western pattern of equal shares may hide variable preferences matching those documented elsewhere. The variability found by Henrich and his colleagues correlates not with demographic variables describing the individuals in the game, but rather, with structural aspects of daily life within the community. Our ideas of fairness are "determined less by the intellectual sphere of our culture than by the way it does business" (Klein 2014, p. 123).

For example, Henrich and his colleagues contrast the Ache of Paraguay with another hunter-gather society, the Hadza in Tanzania.

> Similarly, in Paraguay the Ache regularly share meat. During this sharing, the hunters responsible for the catch commonly forgo their share, while the prey is distributed equally among all other households. There is no consistent relationship between the amount a hunter brings back and the amount his family receives. Successful hunters often leave their prey outside the camp to be discovered by others, carefully avoiding any hint of boastfulness. When asked to divide the Ultimatum Game pie, Ache proposers may have perceived themselves as dividing the game they or a male member of their family had acquired, thereby leading 79 percent of the Ache proposers to offer either half or 40 percent, and 16 percent to offer more than 50 percent, with no rejected offers.
>
> By contrast, the low offers and high rejection rates of the Hadza, another group of small-scale foragers, are not surprising in the light of numerous ethnographic descriptions of these people. Although the Hadza extensively share meat (and other foods to a lesser degree), they do not do so without complaint; many look for opportunities to avoid sharing. Hunters sometimes wait on the outskirts of camp until nightfall so they can sneak meat into their shelter without being seen. It seems the Hadza share because they fear the social consequences that would result from not sharing. Cooperation and sharing is enforced by a fear of punishment that comes in the form of informal social sanctions, gossip, and ostracism. Many Hadza proposers attempted to avoid sharing in the game [the modal offer was 20 percent] and many of them were punished by rejection [24 percent of offers were rejected]. Thus, we find two foraging peoples—the Ache and the Hadza—at opposite ends of the Ultimatum Game spectrum in both proposers' offers and responders' rejections; their contrasting behaviors seem to reflect their differing patterns of everyday life, not any underlying logic of hunter-gatherer life ways (Henrich et al. 2004, pp. 39–40, 176).

Relating group differences to varied economic organizations and market integration, the basic insight is twofold. First, all societies, even stingy ones such as the Hadza, possess an idea of what is fair that varies according to the expectations of normal social relationships. Second, while the local standards for what is fair may vary greatly, there appears to be more consensus concerning what is unfair. There was a level below which the Ache would not generally go, a line below which, when crossed, the offers were routinely rejected even by the Hadza.

5.4 Reconstructing Malinowski's Theory of Law

The Ultimatum Game provides the tools to show how fairness can generate the unified system of law envisioned by Malinowski in *Crime and Custom*. A player has the option of rejecting an offer he judges to be unfair. This punitive action cuts against his self-interest because it means he winds up with nothing at all rather than the little offered by the proposer. This willingness to incur a personal cost to punish someone who has violated a norm is called "altruistic punishment", especially when the punishment promises no direct benefits for the punisher. Instead, the sacrifice benefits future interaction partners who enjoy better performance from the deviant (Fehr and Gächter 2002). Costly punishment "has an emotional representation in the brain and thus seems to be a 'hardwired' prerequisite of our social life" (Rockenbach and Milinski 2006). In short, we derive pleasure from punishing the rule-breaker, even at significant cost to ourselves. Brain scans of subjects, especially males, "revealed that (...) people like cooperating with fair opponents but also like punishing unfair opponents", a sex-difference that could explain "a predominant role for males in the maintenance of justice and punishment of norm violation in human societies (Singer et al. 2006, pp. 467–468).

The social purpose of these rejections is suggested by the finding that UG offers defined as unfair were less likely to be rejected when coming from a computer than from a human. This result suggests "that participants had a stronger emotional reaction to unfair offers from humans than to the same offers from a computer" (Sanfrey et al. 2003). It was not the offer itself that offended, but that it was made by someone who should have known better. Norm enforcement through teaching the offending player a lesson appears to be the goal of the rejection and not simply expressing dissatisfaction with the offer.

While these outcomes may be unsurprising when players target partners who have directly been unfair to the subject as in the UG, broader analyses have shown that punishment by third-parties, or those who have only witnessed the violation but were not directly impacted, "is surprisingly strong. It is only slightly weaker than second-party (within group) punishment" (Camerer and Fehr 2004, p. 78; see also Fehr and Fischbacher 2004). We retaliate against known norm breakers even when we have not been directly impacted with almost the same seriousness (and enjoyment) as actual victims.

From the perspective of the innate emotional reaction against violations of fairness expectations, or altruistic punishment, we can reconsider the description of Malinowski's archetypical criminal infraction. In his account the violation of rules governing clan incest provide a parallel anecdote to the norms of canoe building within his account of the civil law. A suicide results from open complaint of a breach of totemic clan exogamy. Kima'i had consorted with his maternal cousin, and although the affair had gone largely unremarked, a rival initiated the crisis by hurling public accusations. Shamed, the boy ascended a palm tree and, after proclaiming the cruelty of his accuser and urging his family to avenge him, threw himself onto the ground sixty feet below (Malinowski 1926, pp. 77–78).

In Malinowski's analysis the crime is the incestuous liaison, and although "nothing arouses a greater horror than the breach of this prohibition", in fact by his own account the community was quite indifferent toward the infraction. It failed to react directly even when forced to acknowledge the violation, compelling the boy "to carry out the punishment himself". From here Malinowski segued into a consideration of several standard anthropological topics from marriage rules to the uses of magic and sorcery to maintain social order. The end result, while surveying a variety of mechanisms for norm enforcement, is unfocused and confusing in that it tells us little about his intended topic, the criminal law, and certainly nothing that helps us to identify how law is qualitatively different from magic, sorcery, and other social techniques of norm enforcement.

The anecdote makes better sense if it is construed not as an example of punishment against the boy, but of altruistic punishment against his accuser. That the victim calls for vengeance speaks to his sense of having been wronged by his public humiliation for behavior the village was prepared to overlook, and about which, even when prodded, it declined to become overly vexed. The several fights that erupted following the suicide arguably relate more to the death than to the affair. In this interpretive light the major infraction at least from the natives' point of view concerned not the breach of exogamy but instead events beginning with the public accusation. Malinowski went astray when he attended more to the formal elements about which he thought the Trobrianders should be concerned, rather than noticing that something else altogether was stirring the pot.

Broken down into these elements, we discern the basic structure of the enforcement of norms that in the literature form the foundation of the criminal justice system. The accuser pushes forward a humiliating claim over the tacit tolerance of the community, forcing an extreme, but socially modeled response. The boy chooses this option—one that Malinowski suggested is not uncommon in this situation but neither is it required—to punish the accuser for acting selfishly in seeking to remove a romantic rival so as to acquire the woman for himself.

It would have been helpful to have additional details about how the resulting frictions between factions played out, and on what violations they focused. But as it stands we have a complete sketch of altruistic punishment: violation provoking an emotional reaction, leading to punishment of the violator at great personal cost and to no personal benefit. In more modern societies this chain of motivations (crime followed by punishment at public expense) serves to capture most of what is meant by criminal law, and accurately distinguishes it from what is commonly thought of as the civil law.

We arrive then at the major statement of the present argument: reciprocity builds upon an innate attention to violations of fairness expectations, and conclusions framed in terms of reciprocity can be reframed as premises about fairness. This generalization applies to Malinowski's model of law as well. While the description of civil law is a straightforward application of reciprocal exchanges, allowing us to accept his account of the civil law without emendation, the account of the criminal law works only if viewed as an event of altruistic punishment. This reinterpretation allows both sections to use the same explanatory element—fairness, which in the one case is viewed from the perspective of reciprocity, and in the other analyzed in terms of altruistic punishment. This result brings the two kinds of law under one theoretical umbrella, and arrives at the outcome Malinowski desired but could not himself achieve in *Crime and Custom*.

5.5 Conclusion

Malinowski's theory of law stands apart from the innumerably various alternatives within the jurisprudential literature. While many would agree that law is a cultural universal, they assert this as a contingent empirical fact rather than a theoretical inevitability. Malinowski's reciprocity-based model is one of the few capable of generating the expectation that the noble institution of law is necessarily shared by all human societies. Those who hold the equality of all peoples a worthy project will need such a theory in perfected form.

An alternative model does exist that grounds law not in an evolved instinct to track fair treatment, but in the ability to inflict punishment on norm violators. Schauer (2015) has newly defended this view originally offered by Bentham and Austin. If sanction serves as the criterion by which to find law, the problem Malinowski endeavored to solve disappears. Identifying law's essence as the force to compel obedience necessarily means that every culture has law, because every society has sticks.

The weakness of making sanction the *sine qua non* of law is twofold. First, it fails to set law meaningfully apart from other means of norm enforcement, such as religion, etiquette, or custom, all of which inflict punishments on violators. The details of the punishments available to these related institutions may but may not differ from those typically expected from legal systems. Schauer (2015, p. 134) does not limit legal sanctions to physical force: "there is no need to think, at least for our purposes here, of shaming and various other reputation-harming penalties as different in kind from prison, fines, civil disabilities, or, for that matter, flogging". Such differences of degree and not of kind, as we saw earlier, provide an unsatisfactory sorting rule for analytic method and conceptual theorizing.

Second, the need for sanction to maintain order increases as society becomes less cohesive. Fragmented social structures lack the "cross-pressures" to create the "'web of group affiliations' that are subject to the calls of both loyalty and enmity. [Individuals or groups—ed. J.D.] are pulled in contrary directions in conflict situations", tending to prevent an excessive pursuit of intragroup disagreement in one direction because such indulgence incurs costs to other loyalties (Barkun 1968, p. 38, quoting Georg Simmel). When sanction does fit Schauer's description by signaling the primary exercise of legal authority, this condition may be because of the atrophy of other social forces such as family and religion. In such dysfunctional environments law has become distorted through the need to deal with all questions of deviance using the only remaining tool at its disposal. Such a bloated example of "law" should not serve as exemplar of the category, and thus its description falters as a general account of law.

Malinowski's theory is therefore the best foundation on which to construct a defense of the equal dignity of all peoples. To achieve this goal several weaknesses in the original attempt needed remedy. This paper reframes Malinowski's linkage of law and reciprocity as a special instance of the inherent human attention to fairness. When viewed from this more elemental concept, the principle benefit of Malinowski's formulation is preserved—law remains a cultural universal—but all forms of law—not only civil and criminal, but also international—can now be captured within a uniform model.

The result is jurisprudentially unique. From this perspective no special effort is required for a human society to create law (contrary to legal positivists and social contractarians), nor are societies expected to arrive at the same idea of legal norms (contrary to natural law theorists). Further, the crux of law is not mere norm enforcement; other social institutions perform that same task, albeit in different ways. The distinctive work of law as a social institution is to enforce rules in such a manner that the actor accepts the outcome as fair and acceptable, or at least tolerable, even when personally disadvantageous. Only in this way can societies become stable and sustainable in the midst of a reality of social and economic inequality.

References

Andreoni, J., and L. Vesterlund. 2001. Which is the fair sex? Gender differences in altruism. *Quarterly Journal of Economics* 116(1): 293–312.

Ayres, B.D. 1997. Jury decides Simpson must pay $25 million in punitive award. *New York Times* 11 February:A1.

Barash, D.P. 2010. The fairness instinct: Biological roots of today's anger. *Chronicle of Higher Education* 56(40): B8–B10.

Barkun, M. 1968. *Law without sanctions: Order in primitive societies and the world community*. New Haven: Yale University Press.

Becker, L.C. 1986. *Reciprocity*. Chicago: University of Chicago Press.

Beckoff, M. 2004. Wild justice, cooperation, and fair play: Minding manners, being nice, and feeling good. In *The origins and nature of sociality*, ed. R. Sussman and A. Chapman, 53–80. New York: de Gruyter.

Berrey, E., S.G. Hoffman, and L.B. Nielsen. 2012. Situated justice: A contextual analysis of fairness and inequality in employment discrimination litigation. *Law and Society Review* 46 (1): 1–36.

Bloom, P. 2013. *Just babies: The origins of good and evil*. New York: Crown.

Bowles, S., and H. Gintis. 2011. *A cooperative species: Human reciprocity and its evolution*. Princeton: Princeton University Press.

Brosnan, S.F. 2006. Nonhuman species' reactions to inequity and their implications for fairness. *Social Justice Research* 19(2): 153–185.

Brosnan, S.F., and F.B.M. de Waal. 2003. Monkeys reject unequal pay. *Nature* 425(6955): 297–299.

Brosnan, S.F., H.C. Schiff, and F.B.M. de Waal. 2006. Tolerance for inequity may increase with social closeness in chimpanzees. *Proceedings of the Royal Society B* 272(1560): 253–258.

Brunker, M. 2011. *Unable to pay child support, poor parents land behind bars*. http://www.nbcnews.com/id/44376665/ns/us_news-crime_and_courts/t/unable-pay-child-support-poor-parents-land-behind-bars/#.U_zTj2MxIaB [14 April 2014].
Buss, D. 2014. *Evolutionary psychology: The new science of the mind*. London: Pearson.
Camerer, C.F., and E. Fehr. 2004. Measuring social norms and preferences using experimental games: A guide for social scientists. In *Foundations of human sociality*, ed. J. Henrich, R. Boyd, S. Bowles, C. Camerer, E. Fehr, and H. Gintis, 55–95. Oxford: Oxford University Press.
Cheney, D.L., and R.M. Seyfarth. 1990. *How monkeys see the world*. Chicago: University of Chicago Press.
Conley, J., and W. O'Barr. 2002. Back to the Trobriands: The enduring influence of Malinowski's *Crime and custom in savage society*. *Law and Social Inquiry* 27(4): 847–874.
Cosmides, L., and J. Tooby. 2013. Evolutionary psychology: New perspectives on cognition and motivation. *Annual Review of Psychology* 64: 201–229.
de Waal, F.B.M. 2009. *The age of empathy*. London: Souvenir Press.
Donovan, J.M. 2013. Introduction. In *Crime and custom in savage society*, ed. B. Malinowski, 1–15. New Brunswick: Transaction Publishers.
Fehr, E., and U. Fischbacher. 2004. Third-party punishment and social norms. *Evolution and Human Behavior* 25(2): 63–87.
Fehr, E., and S. Gächter. 2002. Altruistic punishment in humans. *Nature* 415(6868): 137–140.
Finkel, N.J. 2001. *Not fair! The typology of commonsense unfairness*. Washington: American Psychological Association.
Freeman, H. 2013. Check your privilege! Whatever that means. *Guardian* (June 5):6.
Gagarin, M. 1986. *Early Greek law*. Berkeley: University of California Press.
Griffith, D.R. 2001. *Animal minds: Beyond cognition to consciousness*. Chicago: University of Chicago Press.
Hartland, E.S. 1924. *Primitive law*. London: Methuen.
Hauser, M.D., M.K. Chen, F. Chen, and E. Chuang. 2003. Give unto others: Genetically unrelated cotton-top tamarin monkeys preferentially give food to those who altruistically give food back. *Proceedings of the Royal Society B* 270(1531): 2363–2370.
Heinrich, H. 1999. *Mind of the raven*. New York: Cliff Street Books.
Henrich, J., R. Boyd, S. Bowles, C. Camerer, E. Fehr, and H. Gintis (eds.). 2004. *Foundations of human sociality: Economic experiments and ethnographic evidence from fifteen small-scale societies*. Oxford: Oxford University Press.
Jensen, K., B. Hare, J. Call, and M. Tomasello. 2006. What's in it for me? Self-regard precludes altruism and spite in chimpanzees. *Proceedings of the Royal Society B* 273(1589): 1013–1021.
Klein, S. 2014. *Survival of the nicest: How altruism made us human and why it pays to get along*. New York: The Experiment.
Kolm, S.-C. 2008. *Reciprocity: An economics of social relations*. Cambridge: Cambridge University Press.
Leslie, T.E.C. 1879. *Essays in political and moral philosophy*. London: Longmans.
Llewellyn, K.N., and E.A. Hoebel. 1941. *The Cheyenne way: Conflict and case law in primitive jurisprudence*. Norman: University of Oklahoma Press.
LoBue, V., T. Nishida, C. Chiong, J.S. DeLoache, and J. Haidt. 2011. When getting something good is bad: Even three-year-olds react to inequality. *Social Development* 20(1): 154–170.
Malinowski, B. 1922. *Argonauts of the western Pacific*. New York: E.P. Dutton & Co.
Malinowski, B. 1926. *Crime and custom in savage society*. London: Routledge and Kegan Paul.
Malinowski, B. 1934. Introduction. In *Law and order in Polynesia*, ed. H. Hogbin, xvii–lxxii. New York: Harcourt Brace.
Malinowski, B. 1939. The group and the individual in functional analysis. *American Journal of Sociology* 44(6): 938–964.
Malinowski, B. 1942. A new instrument for the interpretation of law—Especially primitive. *Yale Law Journal* 51(8): 1237–1254.

Mauss, M. 1967. In *The gift: Forms and functions of exchange in archaic societies*, ed. I. Cunnison. New York: W.W. Norton.
McCabe, K. 2003. *What is the ultimatum game?* http://neuroeconomics.typepad.com/neuroeconomics/2003/09/what_is_the_ult.html [14 April 2016].
Nader, L. 2002. *The life of the law: Anthropological projects*. Berkeley: University of California Press.
Paciotti, B., C. Hadley, C. Holmes, and M. Borgerhoff Mulder. 2005. Grass-roots justice in Tanzania. *American Scientist* 93(1): 58–65.
Pfaff, D.W. 2007. *The neuroscience of fair play*. New York: Dana Press.
Posner, R.A. 1985. An economic theory of the criminal law. *Columbia Law Review* 85(6): 1193–1231.
Post, P., A. Post, L. Post, and D.P. Senning. 2011. *Emily Post's etiquette: Manners for a new world*, 18th ed. New York: William Morrow.
Radcliffe-Brown, A.R. 1952. *Structure and function in primitive society*. New York: Free Press.
Rockenbach, B., and M. Milinski. 2006. The efficient interaction of indirect reciprocity and costly punishment. *Nature* 444(7120): 718–723.
Sahlins, M. 1972. *Stone age economics*. London: Tavistock.
Sanfrey, A.G., J.K. Rilling, J.A. Aronson, L.E. Nystrom, and J.D. Cohen. 2003. The neural basis of economic decision-making in the ultimatum game. *Science* 300(5626): 1755–1758.
Schacter, D.L., D.T. Gilbert, and D.M. Wegner. 2009. *Psychology*. New York: Worth Publishers.
Schauer, F. 2015. *The force of law*. Cambridge: Harvard University Press.
Schiavone, A. 2002. *Invention of law in the west*. Cambridge: Belknap Press.
Silk, J.B., S.F. Brosnan, J. Vonk, J. Henrich, D.J. Povinelli, A.S. Richardson, S.P. Lambeth, J. Mascaro, and S.J. Schapiro. 2005. Chimpanzees are indifferent to the welfare of unrelated group members. *Nature* 437(7063): 1357–1359.
Singer, T., B. Seymour, J.P. O'Doherty, K.E. Stephan, R.J. Dolan, and C.D. Frith. 2006. Empathic neural responses are modulated by the perceived fairness of others. *Nature* 439(7075): 466–469.
Stępień, M. 2010. The question of nonhuman primates morality. In *Studies in the philosophy of law, Vol. 5: law and biology*, ed. J. Stelmach, B. Brożek, and M. Soniewicka, 135–153. Kraków: Jagiellonian University Press.
Tamanaha, B.Z. 1993. The folly of the "social scientific" concept of legal pluralism. *Journal of Law and Society* 20(2): 192–217.
Texas Appleseed. 2014. *Complaint to Richard Cordray, Director, Consumer Financial Protection Bureau*. http://big.assets.huffingtonpost.com/Complaint3.pdf [15 April 2016].
Tinklepaugh, O.L. 1928. An experimental study of representative factors in monkeys. *Journal of Comparative Psychology* 8(3): 197–236.
Tyler, T. 2006. *Why people obey the law*. Princeton: Princeton University Press.
Weber, M. 1954. *Law in economy and society*. Cambridge: Harvard University Press.
Wolgast, E. 1987. *The grammar of justice*. Ithaca: Cornell University Press.
Yan, Y. 1996. *The flow of gifts: Reciprocity and social networks in a Chinese village*. Stanford: Stanford University Press.

The manufacturer's authorised representative in the EU is Springer Nature Customer Service Centre GmbH, Europaplatz 3, 69115 Heidelberg, Germany. If you have any concerns regarding our products, please contact ProductSafety@springernature.com

Printed and bound by CPI Group (UK) Ltd, Croydon, CR0 4YY
22/09/2026
02220950-0014